BEST NEWSPAPER WRITING 1981

odern Media Institute
556 Central Avenue
St. Petersburg, Florida 33701

Other books in this series

BEST NEWSPAPER WRITING

1981

Winners

The American Society
of Newspaper Editors
Competition

Edited by Roy Peter Clark

Acknowledgments

Grateful acknowledgment is made to the
following for permission to reprint the
newspaper articles included in this book:

The Associated Press and Saul Pett
The Los Angeles Herald Examiner and Thomas Plate
The Pine Bluff Commercial and Paul Greenberg
The Seattle Times and Richard Zahler
The Washington Post and Thomas Boswell
The Philadelphia Inquirer and Steve Lovelady

LC Catalog Card No. 80-646604
ISBN 0-935742-03-4
ISSN 0195-895X

Printed in the United States of America

Cover sculpture, illustrations
and vignettes by Joe Tonelli.
Author portraits by Jack Barrett.
Book design by Billie Keirstead.

In memory of Dick Bothwell

About this book

AUGUST, 1981

This is Volume III in what we hope will become a small library of books of and about fine newspaper writing. It is a useful book which is enjoyable reading. It's a "how-to" book and a "hands-on" book which is fun to read.

Volume III is a happy melding of three important ingredients:

The American Society of Newspaper Editors (ASNE)

Roy Peter Clark

The Modern Media Institute (MMI)

ASNE took on the task of giving U.S. and Canadian newspaper readers something better to read in 1977. First it commissioned a study and a widely-distributed report on writing by Roy Peter Clark. Then the Society voted to sponsor and fund a contest to identify the finest writing in newspapers and to reward the winning writers each year.

The selection is made by a panel of editors who meet for several days to read and evaluate the mailbags full of stories. Nineteen editors picked this year's winners from nearly 700 entries in four categories — deadline writing, non-deadline writing, commentary and sports.

The panel was headed by **David Laventhol,** publisher of *Newsday* on Long Island and included:

Judith Brown, *New Britain* (Conn.) *Herald*
Anthony Day, *Los Angeles Times*

James Driscoll, *Boca Raton* (Fla.) *News*
Murray Gart, *Washington Star*
William Giles, *Detroit News*
Harold Gulliver, *Atlanta Constitution*
Robert Haiman, *St. Petersburg Times*
Larry Jinks, *Knight-Ridder Newspapers*
Alex S. Jones, *Greeneville* (Tenn.) *Sun*
James B. King, *Seattle Times*
David Lawrence, *Detroit Free Press*
Richard Leonard, *Milwaukee Journal*
Maxwell McCrohon, *Chicago Tribune*
Ed Murray, *Boulder* (Colo.) *Camera*
Joe Murray, *Lufkin* (Texas) *News*
Marjorie Paxson, *Chambersburg* (Pa.)
Public Opinion
Fred Taylor, *Wall Street Journal*
Thomas Winship, *Boston Globe.*

Contest winners receive $1,000 awards at the annual convention of the Society, which has a membership of nearly 900 newspaper editors in the United States and Canada. Since its founding by a handful of editors in 1922, ASNE has become the most prestigious organization of men and women who control the news and editorial content of America's daily newspapers.

Without the ASNE contest there obviously would be no *Best Newspaper Writing 1981.* But a second very important ingredient is the editor of Volume III (and of Volume I and Volume II), **Roy Peter Clark.**

Although only 33, Clark was among the first "writing coaches" and has become a sort of guru among those dedicated to better newspaper writing. He earned his Ph.D. in English from the State University of New York and moved into newspapering from the English faculty at Auburn University.

Eugene C. Patterson, editor and president of *The St. Petersburg Times* and in 1977 president of ASNE, asked Clark to direct a writing project for *The Times* and the Society — and that is where it all began.

Clark is now on the staff of the Modern Media Institute where in addition to editing *Best Newspaper Writing* he organizes and directs writing seminars for newspaper men and women.

The third ingredient is Modern Media Institute which serves as coordinator of the writing contest and is the non-profit publisher of this series of books.

The Institute was founded in 1975 by the late Nelson Poynter, chairman of *The St. Petersburg Times* and *Congressional Quarterly* in Washington. On his death in 1978 Poynter bequeathed stock in *The Times* to MMI, which spends its dividends on projects such as this and others which include:

Roy Peter Clark's writing seminars.

Media management courses for professionals and for graduate students.

Special newspaper writing courses for liberal arts students interested in writing for publication.

A program to identify and encourage minority high school students interested in writing and journalism.

The creation of a modern typographical laboratory for the production of student newspapers.

Some weeks ago a journalism professor in Kansas wrote:

"Your collection of the 1980 winners is the only usable textbook for reporting I have found."

Volume III will be just as usable, and just as readable, for all teachers and students, for writers and editors and for readers who enjoy fine writing.

Donald K. Baldwin
Director
Modern Media Institute

Contents

Introduction

MAY, 1981

A small group of newspaper writers came to St. Petersburg last February, sat for five days around a conference table, and talked about why the craft they love seems at times so frustrating. The writing seminar was in its fourth day when a lull in the conversation suggested that even these garrulous writers had run out of things to say.

Just then Dave Behrens, a fine feature writer with *Newsday,* put the collective contemplation into words. "When you write something you love," he said, "it dies so soon."

That cold reality, faced by every journalist who considers himself a writer, violates all ancient traditions of literary language. Perhaps Shakespeare could say with confidence to his lover: "So long as men can breathe, or eyes can see,/So long lives this, and this gives life to thee." If the Bard had worn a green eyeshade, he might have said something like "So long, farewell, these words I've writ today,/And now it's time to go collect my pay."

How frustrating to write for a medium in which most words die in a day. "I've written 17 million words over the years," my friend Ray Jenkins, editor of the *Clearwater Sun,* once said to me. "That's enough to fill half the *Encyclopedia Britannica.* And here and there I might even clip out a piece and save it in the vain hope that somebody might want to read it some day."

Perhaps it is this transitory nature of the craft which has bequeathed us a necrology of newspaper writing, a language of death. Reporters write on *deadline*. Editors hold meetings called *post-mortems*. Old stories are kept in a *morgue*. Editors *kill* stories (how true).

Language reflects attitudes, and in some cases determines them. The jargon of journalism reveals much about the values and perceptions of generations of writers and editors.

Take the hideous newspaper noun *brite*. That's spelled b-r-i-t-e. For years the only interesting writing, the only humor, the only relief from the banality of daily American journalism was in something called the six-inch brite.

Conversation overheard in newsroom:

"I've got space for a six-inch brite."

"How about several 20-inch dulls?"

Consider the language we use to describe the effects of newspaper writing on the reader. I once heard a city editor say something like: "The lead should have a news hook and should grab the reader and be filled with buzz words. Then, after the jump, there should be a kicker at the end."

Pity the poor reader. All she wants is to relax with her newspaper. All we want is to grab, hook, buzz, jump and kick her.

Talk to students about what writing teachers do to their papers and inevitably the language has connotations of violence. "He tore up my paper." "She ripped it to shreds." "He bled all over it in red ink." "All she does is cut up my work." What do editors do to stories in the cant of the newspaper world? Editors cut them, spike them, kill them and bounce them back. Nothing in the language suggests cooperation, consultation, instruction or teamwork. A young writer hands in a flawed story, looking for guidance. What happens? It bounces back.

Listen to the language some editors use to evaluate the work of writers:

If the work is bad: "This really stinks."

If the work is good: "I can't see anything wrong with it."

If the work is excellent: "Looks OK to me."

It is ironic that some men and women who produce millions of words a year for publication lack a useful critical vocabulary for understanding, evaluating and improving their work.

You need not be a student of formal rhetoric to write well. You don't have to know synecdoche from Schenectady, an oxymoron from a water buffalo, or a zeugma from a zipper.

Some of my best writers are fifth-graders at Bay Point Elementary School. I teach writing there one morning a week. No one has to teach 11-year-old Bonnie Harris about parallelism, variety of sentence length, significant detail, economy of style or emphatic word order. She knows it. She's a writer.

But as she grows in her craft, she will also become more articulate about the process of writing, just like the great foul shooter who can break down his skill into its smallest parts. Eyes on the rim. Knees bent. Elbows in. Deep breath. Up on the toes. Follow through with the wrist. Rotation on the ball. Swish. Most people can make a few foul shots without thinking about any of this. Those at the top of the craft understand form and technique.

As you might expect, the writers represented in this year's edition of *Best Newspaper Writing* are wonderfully articulate about what they do. Saul Pett of the *Associated Press* knows he may have to write a dozen bad metaphors before he comes up with the perfect one he needs. Richard Zahler of the *Seattle Times* knows how to create suspense in a long narrative, even when the readers know the outcome of the story. Thomas Boswell of the *Washington Post* knows he must find the central thread of the story, that logical line upon which he can hang his best details, quotations, description and anecdotes. Thomas Plate of the *Los Angeles Herald Examiner* may only have an hour to write an important political story, but he knows how to prepare his emotions and intellect to take advantage of every second of his available time. Paul Greenberg of the *Pine Bluff* (Ark.) *Commercial* knows that to please himself and his readers he must get his words into just the right rhythm, and to do that he must be ready to rewrite, rewrite, rewrite.

Using all their skills, these writers have produced the 13 prize-winning stories in this collection. We see the ethnic and political splendor of New York City Mayor Ed Koch; the self-reliant communities of Washington State react to the disaster of Mt. St. Helens; Carter and Kennedy struggle for political power at the Democratic National Convention; a great Southern newspaper is sold; the Phillies win the World Series; the American dream blurs during an election year in Thomas Wolfe's Asheville, North Carolina; two great boxers battle for a world championship; a writer meditates on a Florida beach; Southern demagogue Orval Faubus is remembered; hometown boy Ronald Reagan makes good. It's hard to imagine a group of stories that better reflects the diversity of journalistic interests, or one that is more typically American.

If these stories are compelling in their diversity, so are the writers. The youngest is 34, the oldest is 63. They represent a wire service, big newspapers, and a small one. They live on the East Coast, West Coast, and in Arkansas. Saul Pett outlines his working material, but not his story. Paul Greenberg outlines his story, but not his working material. Thomas Plate and Thomas Boswell never use outlines when writing on deadline. Richard Zahler always does. Boswell and Zahler love the new computer terminals. Greenberg refuses to use one. Pett still writes on a typewriter and occasionally on a cocktail napkin.

Despite these differences, Pett, Boswell, Zahler, Plate and Greenberg share values which identify them as writers. They love the English language, its proper and creative use. They can tell a good story. They believe writing is rewriting. They recognize that good writing depends on good reporting. They have faith in their audience. They have an eye for the people who will make good stories. They have an ear for the right word in the right place.

The readers of *Best Newspaper Writing 1981*

will have the chance to discover these writers and their values for themselves. The book has been redesigned to better serve the growing number of reporters, editors, teachers and students who have embraced the *Best Newspaper Writing* series in the last three years.

Stories: Each writer submitted five stories to the ASNE Distinguished Writing competition. Of these winning stories, we have selected at least two from each writer. The stories include news, features, sports, news analysis, commentary, essays. Some were written under oppressive deadlines, others were developed at a more leisurely pace. We have tried to select "the best of the best." But we also have considered subject and length so as to offer the most useful models for students and working journalists. All the stories were written in 1980.

Discussions: There are few more useful exercises for the student of writing than to listen to skilled writers talk about the writing process. I interviewed each writer by telephone for up to two hours, and each conversation was an education for me. The interviews were transcribed and edited for brevity and clarity. They should start students thinking about the way they write. Teachers may want to use them to develop writing exercises and class discussion.

Questions and observations: This new section follows each story. We hope it will make the book more useful for classes in newspaper writing.

> *This section makes hard critical judgments about the stories and invites the reader to cultivate his own critical faculties.
> *It tests these newspaper stories against the most rigorous literary standards.
> *It raises important questions for individual thought and group discussion.
> *It recognizes that good writing comes from good reading and suggests further reading for the student.

*It offers some writing projects that these stories inspire.

We hope that *Best Newspaper Writing* will continue to be an impetus in the national movement to improve newspaper writing. It will not be easy. To fill our newspapers with good writing, editors will have to become teachers in the newsroom, and teachers will have to become editors in the classroom. Perhaps this book can help.

In any case, it will prove to doubters that you can be a writer and work for a newspaper. We can't promise literary immortality even to Pett, Boswell, Zahler, Plate and Greenberg. But at least this volume—and the work of the American Society of Newspaper Editors—guarantees that their stories will rest on desks and book shelves to be encountered by students and journalists for some years to come. The words may die eventually, but not so soon.

Roy Peter Clark
St. Petersburg, Florida

BEST NEWSPAPER WRITING 1981

Saul Pett
Non-Deadline Writing

SAUL PETT's byline is well known to American newspaper readers. He is one of seven AP reporters designated as special correspondents. Pett works out of AP Newsfeatures in New York, but he travels all over the world tracking down good stories. His previous work has taken him to such mysterious places as the South Pole, Hudson Bay and Washington, D.C., the most mysterious of all. He was born in Passaic, N.J., in 1918 and received a journalism degree from the University of Missouri. He was fired from his first newspaper job at the *New York Daily News* "because the city editor didn't care for copy boys learning to be rewrite men." He joined the Associated Press in 1946 after working for International News Service in Detroit, Chicago, and New York.

Koch grabs Big Apple
and shakes it

NOVEMBER 30, 1980

NEW YORK (AP) — He is the freshest thing to blossom in New York since chopped liver, a mixed metaphor of a politician, the antithesis of the packaged leader, irrepressible, candid, impolitic, spontaneous, funny, feisty, independent, uncowed by voter blocs, unsexy, unhandsome, unfashionable and altogether charismatic, a man oddly at peace with himself in an unpeaceful place, a mayor who presides over the country's largest Babel with unseemly joy.

Clearly, an original. Asked once what he thought his weaknesses were, Ed Koch said that for the life of him he couldn't think of any. "I like myself," he said.

The streets are still dirty. The subways are still unsafe. The specter of bankruptcy is never farther away than next year's loan. But Edward Irving Koch, who runs the place like a solicitous Jewish mother with no fear of the rich relatives, appears to be the most popular mayor of this implausible town since Fiorello LaGuardia more than a generation ago.

He is a Democrat, an excommunicated liberal, a symptom of his time, the leader of a city traditionally in the vanguard of the country's troubles.

Long before the conservative convulsion changed the face of national government this month, Ed Koch offended traditional liberals by being the mayor who says no to a variety of causes, by speaking constantly of the limits of government, by seeking to restore what he calls a balance between the rights and needs of the majority and those of the minorities, the rights of the victim and those of the accused.

But more than programs or policies, it is per-

sonality that makes this mayor special. He is
seltzer with a lifetime fizz. When other Democrats were prostrated by the Reagan sweep, Ed
Koch was genially philosophic.

"If God wanted us to have life tenure," he
said, "he would have made all of us federal
judges."

Every day of this year's 11-day transit
strike, rain or shine, Koch stationed himself near
the Manhattan end of the Brooklyn Bridge ap-
plauding the commuters on foot. "Thank you for
being strong," he sang out. "Thank you for coming to work." The sight was so undoing that some
of the reluctant hikers found themselves saying,
"Oh, you're welcome. It's our pleasure."

Dedicating a new shopping mall in Brooklyn, Koch was well launched into his theme
("New York is on the way back") when one of the
many blacks in the audience yelled, "We want
John Lindsay."

Koch paused at this reference to the former
mayor, who stood high with the blacks. "Everybody who wants Lindsay back," he said, "raise
their hands." Some hands went up. Whereupon,
hizzoner leaned forward like a scolding school
teacher and roared, "DUMMIES!" The crowd
loved it. Koch beamed like a kosher pumpkin.

Other mayors have complained about the
burdens of the job, the second most difficult in the
country, goes the cliche. Not this mayor. He
thrives on the tumult, the contention, the push
and pull and what he calls the immediacy of his
constituents. No other job brings a leader so close
to the people, he says, citing a piquant reason.

"If you want to picket the governor, it costs
you $18 to go to Albany. If you want to picket the
president, it costs you $60 to go to Washington.
But if you want to picket the mayor of New York,
it costs you only 60 cents, subway or bus. And believe me, they picket."

But picket legally they must or Koch throws
them out. He suffers no guff, regardless of race,
creed, or color. He refuses to be a punching bag

for pressure groups. His bluntness is ecumenical; at one time or another he has angered whites and blacks, Jews and Gentiles, management and labor.

In 1978, his first year in office, he received a group of black ministers at City Hall. They demanded that all summer federal jobs go to non-whites. Koch said that's illegal, the program is based on poverty and "there are some poor whites, you know."

The ministers said unless Koch yielded to their demand they would sit outside his office, sing and let no one in or out. Koch said they could sing all they wanted outside of City Hall. They wouldn't leave. Koch told the nearest cop to remove them. "What if they resist?" asked the cop. "Have you never heard the word, ARREST?" said the mayor. The ministers were arrested and Koch never again had trouble with illegal demonstrations within City Hall.

In his third month in office, Koch went to a large meeting of white, middle-class constituents at a Catholic high school in Queens, where his administration was to be put on "trial." Koch asked if he could have two minutes for opening remarks. The presiding priest said he could have one minute. Koch said in that case he was leaving, and left.

"Now, nobody walks out on 1,100 Irish and Italian Catholics in a church setting," the mayor recalled. "Somebody asked me, how can you do this? I said, you don't treat me with respect, I walk out. They've got a kangaroo court in there and I don't happen to be a kangaroo."

In 1978, some 3,000 Chassidic Jews, infuriated by the murder of an elderly member of the sect, stormed a Brooklyn police station and held it for a time. Koch expressed sympathy for the victim but delivered a stern lecture to the effect that no one, but no one, has the right to seize a police station. That earned him enmity among some members of his own religion.

More recently, the mayor was asked at a discussion group in a synagogue if he could think of any great leaders in the world today. "Anwar Sadat," said Koch. The audience booed. "Oh, stop the booing already, don't be ridiculous," said hizzoner, going on to extol the courage of the Egyptian president.

The mayor has outraged civil libertarians by advocating the death penalty for murder, by berating judges who impose lenient bail (in one case, the accused proved innocent), by calling for a revamping and speeding up of the criminal justice system, which lawyer Koch says, succinctly, "stinks."

His pursuit of the lawless has been known to be personal and relentless. In 1971, Koch, then a member of Congress, was braced by a black man in a Manhattan park and threatened with mayhem unless he gave him a quarter. ("He was 6-feet-3, and every time I tell the story he gets bigger.")

Koch refused and threatened the stranger with arrest. The man looked at Koch as if he were crazy and ran off. In the distance, Koch saw him succeed in getting coins from two other people. A block later, Koch found a police car and demanded that the cops find the menacing panhandler. The cops said that would take time. Let's take the time, Koch said, even though he was already late for a banquet of Jewish constituents.

Ultimately, in the ensuing hours, the culprit was nabbed, brought into court (where an assistant district attorney tried vainly to dissuade Koch from pursuing such a small matter), fined $50 for harassment and, claiming he was employed but broke at the moment, was given three weeks to pay.

Three weeks later, still in pursuit, Koch wrote the court clerk asking if the fine had been paid. No answer. Six weeks later, he tried again and was told the defendant had failed to pay the fine, a warrant was out for his arrest but he couldn't be found, having given a false name and address.

"I said you don't know his right name. You don't know where he lives and you issued a warrant for his arrest! Hah, hah, hah. And I realized how screwed up our court system was."

The mayor of New York is 56, a bachelor, tall, fit and quick (last year he wrestled an egg-throwing heckler to the floor before the cops could move.) His face—it must be the most un-poker face in politics today—is framed by a bald pate and wispy sideburns and seems never in repose. His voice, like his face, is never without expression. He talks in sing-song, allegro, andante, fortissimo, pianissimo, and in the crescendos of emphasis he stretches out syllables in capital letters. When he says, ONE BILL-Y-ON-DOLL-ARS, you can see the whole pile, in singles.

Like presidents, governors and other mayors around the country, Koch finds that bureaucracy is a "colossus that sits and sits and you have to push and push. The civil servants know there isn't a thing you can do about getting rid of them; they're all going to be here long after you're gone." So, he pushes.

On Jan. 20, 1978, Koch's 20th day in office, he was awakened at three in the morning by a call from the city's personnel director.

"Mr. Mayor, it's snowing."

Koch thought that was a novel way to get the news.

"So?"

"Do you want me to declare a Snow Day?"

"What does that mean?"

"A Snow Day means that when a city employee comes in to work he gets time-and-a-half. If they don't come in, they get paid anyway."

"Henceforth, in the city of New York, there will be NO more Snow Days."

The snow that day was the heaviest in 10 years. There were two more snowstorms that month. By not declaring them, the mayor's office calculates, the city saved $8.5 million. New York, which struggles along on an annual budget of $13 billion, the third largest in American gov-

ernment, employs 250,000 people.

On one of his walks around town, Koch was handed a note by a constituent: "The volleyball nets in Central Park are six inches too high. They're screwed up."

The mayor passed the note along to the appropriate bureaucrat with orders that, if the nets were as described, "unscrew them." After some days of cost analysis, that underling reported back that the posts holding the volleyball nets would have to be pulled up at high cost. "Why," asked the mayor "do you have to pull up the posts? Just untie the nets and lower them." Eureka! It was done.

Koch thinks Ronald Reagan won big because people are fed up with the heavy hand and the high cost of government. He calls himself a "liberal with sanity" as opposed to traditional liberals who thought they could solve problems by throwing money at them. He now regrets that for nine years in Congress, he was one of the money-throwers.

With others, he voted for a law requiring cities to make mass transit equally accessible to the handicapped.

"Sounds terrific, doesn't it? But do you know what that MEANS? It means that in New York City we would have to spend over a BILL-Y-ON-DOLL-ARS—the federal government doesn't provide dollar one—for elevators and other things so that people in wheel chairs could use the subways. For the number who'd use them, that comes to $50 a ride. We say we'll take them wherever they want to go by limousine. It would be cheaper."

The government also insists that the city provide special classes for emotionally and physically handicapped children. For this, the feds provide $8.5 million.

"So go do it. But the added cost is $300 million. Where is the money going to come from? From the police, the firemen, sanitation, corrections? WHERE?"

The mayor's voice, now at a high screech, descends into quiet reality. "People understand that being told to do good things, when you can't afford them, is not doing good things. There are no free lunches. SOMEBODY pays, and that's what the election was all about."

On matters of race and equality before the law, the mayor says that racism can be a two-way street, that discrimination is not solved by reverse discrimination, that there are "black rednecks as well as white rednecks," that the rights of society must be paramount.

He cites the case of a black man arrested on the complaint of a woman who said he twice shoved her onto the tracks of a subway. Out on the street of a quiet residential area, the man fights and screams as two cops attempt to handcuff him. Windows go up. Somebody yells, "Stop that police brutality!"

That, the mayor says, is symptomatic of the "liberal syndrome." Too many people, he says, have indulged in self-flagellation and guilt over matters of race.

"I am not guilt-ridden. My father was not a slave holder. (Louis Koch, a Polish immigrant to New York, worked in the fur business by day and a hat-check concession at night during the Depression.) We were poor. (Nine people in a two-bedroom walkup.) I want to help poor people, right?

"But you don't help them by pandering or preferential treatment. I'm against racial quotas in employment. I am for affirmative action in which you reach out and say, come, come if you don't have the skills we'll teach you. But when you take the test, you take it EQUALLY with EVERYBODY."

Edward Irving Koch loves his job but says a mayor without a sense of humor would go out of his skull. Thus, this mayor threw up his hands in roaring, laughing futility when told that illegal street peddlers were now using merchandise racks two feet too long for the police vans used to confiscate them.

He goes around town telling people that he intends—he doesn't say hopes—to be mayor for three terms, 12 years. "If you happen to throw me out at the end of four years," he says, in his sing-song way, with the certitude of a man dealing with unassailable reality, "I'll get a better job but you won't get a better mayor."

Observations and questions

1) Editors for years have been preaching the virtue of short leads: one sentence, 18 words. Readability studies also extol the short sentence. Saul Pett's lead is one sentence—65 words long. Why does this sentence work? How is it possible for such a long sentence to be readable and interesting? Examine its syntax.

2) Some would describe the first sentence as a *cumulative* sentence. Subject and verb come first. Then follows a long series of modifiers. Imitate the structure of this sentence in describing a colorful person whom you know, perhaps a teacher or a friend.

3) The best writers work with both long and short sentences. Study Pett's style. What effect does the long sentence have on the reader? The short sentence? In the first three paragraphs, what effect does Pett create by varying the length of his sentences?

4) An essential playfulness runs through the work of most good writers, a love for the language in which words hug and bump each other. Pett uses several images—metaphors and similes—to create a picture of Koch. Discuss the appropriateness of each:

> The intentional mixed metaphor in the first sentence.
> "...who runs the place like a solicitous Jewish mother."
> "He is seltzer with a lifetime fizz."
> The musical analogy that describes the mayor's voice.
> "Koch beamed like a kosher pumpkin."

5) Quotations make this piece come alive. How does Pett use the Koch quotations in the story? Examine their placement.

6) Quotations help amplify some important anecdotes. Discuss the placement of these anecdotes and how they contribute to your knowledge of the mayor's character.

7) Teachers of writing often say something like "Show, don't tell." In which passages does Pett tell us about Koch? In which does he show us about the mayor? How do these passages complement each other?

8) Go back and read a personality profile you've written or one that has appeared in a local newspaper. Have you learned anything from reading Pett's story that you could have used to improve this profile?

The folks in Asheville — turned off and tuned out

MAY 25, 1980

ASHEVILLE, North Carolina — "Buy American?" snorts a perfectly good American. "Why should I?"

"Half this country keeps the other half going," says a bitter housewife in line at the checkout counter. Ahead of her is a man buying more meat than she can afford. He pays with food stamps.

"We can't do anything about those crazy Iranians holding our people," writes a rural editorialist, "but we can do something about taxes. We can control them."

"I'm relatively affluent but will I be able to send my kids to college?" asks the executive director of what used to be a pillar of American optimism, the local Chamber of Commerce.

"The election?" ponders an old mountaineer. "I ain't heard it mentioned except on the TV."

Something is wrong, Jimmy, Teddy, Ronnie, Georgie and Johnny, and you ain't reaching them. If this part of the country is any barometer, America is turned off by the election of 1980. Most people here seem to think that the identity of the next president won't make much difference. He's up there and they're down here, two different worlds that no longer meet.

They don't use the word but they mean the word that used to be heard only from hell-raising college kids. Except in negative ways, they find government irrelevant. More precisely, these Middle Americans find government relevant to their pain, not their pleasure.

Church membership is up. Even the Baptists and the Episcopalians agree on that. Nobody is sure why. "I'm not at all certain it means a greater spirituality," says the Rev. Frederick H.

Dennis of the All Souls Episcopal Church. "Maybe we're getting them by default as they lose faith in government and other institutions."

Malaise, a diagnosis projected by President Carter and other unlicensed sociologists, is not the word for the people of western North Carolina. They are not bent low with immobilizing gloom and doom.

The opening of the trout season, the explosion of the azaleas and dogwoods, in spring, when "even the telephone poles look like they're in bloom," are still festivals of joy. Bluegrass music still packs 'em into the dance halls and beer distributors are not hurting. People are still nourished in their souls by the surrounding grandeur, by the misty mysteries of the Blue Ridge and the Smokies, the mountains that Thomas Wolfe, the best known native son, found "lordly, with a plan."

But inflation gnaws away at their earthly plans and pocketbooks, rising taxes corrode their civility as citizens, and the spectacle of Americans held hostage abroad does profound violence, yet again, to their national pride and sense of reason in the world. Perhaps it's true that the barometer of a nation's dismay may be read by the intensity of its celebrations. Here, as apparently everywhere, Americans cheered loudly, with an exquisite sense of pride and community, over the U.S. Olympic hockey team because recent history has provided so little to cheer about.

If there is a malaise, these people feel, it is not here but in Washington and Detroit, in Houston and other places where, in their perception, leaders are screwing up.

Here, where Thomas Wolfe lived, it is now painful to recall a scene from *Look Homeward Angel*. On the porch of his mother's boarding house, with its grand view of the mountains (now obliterated by a 12-story hotel), among the wood and cane rockers and the slatted gliders hanging from the ceiling, his father is holding forth on the glories of America to a mesmerized group of boarders (who paid $1 for a room and "three square meals" a day):

"And what did we do, gentlemen? We sank their navy in an action that lasted only 20 minutes (and) stormed at by shot and shell, Teddy and his Rough Riders took the hill at Santiago."

There was a spring day near the turn of the century, when the curve of American power in the world was beginning its upward arch. Now, on another spring day 80 years later, at the other end of the curve bent low in national humiliation and frustration, this:

"All day long I've been walking around feeling hopeless and foolish and I can't shake it," said a man in downtown Asheville the day after the rescue of the hostages failed in Iran.

"In the first place, they should've done something much sooner," said Cindi Wyatt, who runs a restaurant in Waynesville, west of Asheville. "In the second place, they shouldn't have screwed it up."

"They" are in government and "they" are in industry, in the litany of grievances people here voice against their leaders.

"We don't expect miracles, we don't expect our leaders to take all of the up-hill out of life," said Dr. Cecil Sherman, pastor of the First Baptist Church, the biggest around. "I'd accept any economic policy that was fair. The irritating thing is the unevenness of the bite.

"It gripes me that the oil industry is getting rich on my pain. It's not only the sheiks in the Mideast but the sheiks in Houston. I don't expect favors from Saudi Arabia but I also don't expect Exxon to rob me.

"And if Detroit had been responsive to our needs, I would now be driving a small American car instead of a Datsun. The leaders in the auto industry could not see what every plumber and bus driver and postman in Asheville saw a long time ago, that we need cars with more gas mileage. So why should I 'buy American'?"

A town of 57,000, richly endowed by nature and partially bleached by man, Asheville rests somewhat restlessly on a high plateau at the confluence of the French Broad and Swannanoa rivers. Its chief industries are tourism, textiles, lumber, paper and furniture. Most of the surrounding farms, which produce tobacco, apples, tomatoes and other vegetables, are small and increasingly more farmers have to moonlight in factories to survive inflation.

The mountains are still here, although one ridge, a happy necking ground in Thomas Wolfe's youth known as Beaucatcher, now bears a shocking gash for an expressway. There has been some pollution of air and stream but much less than elsewhere.

The summers are still cool, mostly in the 70s, making this stretch of North Carolina an attractive part of the Sunbelt, enticing rich Floridians to build summer homes in the mountains while dismayed natives watch the price of land climb even higher. To the west, the Great Smoky

Mountain National Park is still irresistible, so much so that tourists have made it the first national park to require traffic lights. Beauty here, like beauty everywhere these days, brings mixed blessings.

So does change. Merchants followed home buyers in the classic rush to the suburbs, leaving much of downtown Asheville empty or crumbling and the city desperate for tax revenue. An argument rages over whether to spend $35 million to build a big downtown shopping mall in the hope of luring shoppers back.

Crimes of violence are down somewhat but thievery is up. Asheville took longer than much of the nation to lock its doors, but they are locked now. As the price of silver rose, so many housewives were locking up their family silver in banks the banks ran out of large safe deposit boxes. "In the old days," said Nancy Brower, *Asheville Times* columnist, "we had to bury our silver against you Yankees. Now we have our own homegrown thieves."

In the sweep of change, one man's horror becomes another's nostalgia. Trying to go home again, Thomas Wolfe lamented that they were levelling the old, wooden Battery Park Hotel for a 16-story steel and brick building, "stamped out of the same mold, as if by some gigantic biscuit-cutter of hotels that had produced a thousand others like it all over the country."

Fifty years later, by which time the "new" Battery Park Hotel had become a touchstone of his youth, another writer came home to lament that the hotel was being abandoned. Its rooms were too small, its convention facilities too meager to interest any of the chains. It is now being redone as an apartment house.

Historically, North Carolina was the first of the 13 colonies to vote for independence, the next to the last to ratify the Constitution and, in the Civil War, one of four border states which wavered over secession but finally joined the Confederacy. Most of the state's largest plantations

were east of Asheville, which accounts for the
fact that the western part of the state has fewer
blacks and more Republicans.

In party registration, Democrats still out-
number Republicans 3-to-1, a ratio which is more
important in state politics than national. Western North Carolina, largely conservative, went
for Eisenhower and Nixon.

Carter carried the area with ease in 1976,
mostly because he seemed like a nice Southern
boy, but this year is expected to have a closer battle if the opposition is Ronald Reagan. Neither
man is setting this electorate afire. People don't
see much difference between them. People question Carter's competence and Reagan's age and
"impulsiveness."

"I'll have to flip a coin," said Wade Wilson of
Dillsboro, whose own meteoric career in politics
may say more about the mood of voters these
days than either Carter or Reagan. Wilson returned home one night from a Rotary meeting
when his wife said:

"Guess what?"

"What?"

"You've just been elected mayor."

"No way. I wasn't running."

"You won on a write-in vote."

Wilson swept greater Dillsboro, population
194, because the incumbent had the temerity to
talk about raising taxes. He serves now with an
enthusiasm that is explained by the fact that the
job pays nothing and the official duties include
being rousted out of bed at night to unplug a
sewer or fix a water line.

The reluctant mayor works for an oil company and travels every week through seven
counties of western North Carolina, where he
finds people bugged by inflation, apprehensive
about the economy and reluctant, in business
and their private lives, to spend money on anything more than they absolutely need.

"Nothing, nobody is turning people on these
days," he reports. "Everything is turning them

off."

In town and country, inflation saps people's lives and plans like a pernicious anemia and undermines the old American ethic that security awaits those who work hard and save their money.

Mobile homes now mottle the lovely hillsides, shelter for the many who can't afford the price of a conventional house. In Biltmore Park, the rich suburb of Asheville, even doctors and lawyers have begun to buy second-hand clothes in the "Next to New Shop" run by the Junior League.

High up in the mountains, past the yellow ribbons hung from mail boxes and telephone poles for the Americans held captive in Iran, in a place called Canada Township, near where the hardtop runs out, Jesse Brown snaps the galluses over his plaid shirt and holds forth on the nation's economy next to the pot-bellied stove in his small general store.

"People been cussing everybody from the president to the sheriff for high prices. I quit pumping gas and selling coffee cuz I didn't want them cussing on me."

In town and country, people grumble about government, about the high cost of bureaucracy and stifling regulation, about welfare recipients who drive up to supermarkets in big cars and pay with food stamps. City councilmen and county commissioners are shouted down for even mentioning the possibility of a tax hike. In his rage and frustration, one taxpayer at a Burke County meeting whipped out a scissors and cut off the tie of a county commissioner.

In 1980, in the United States of America, said a recent editorial in the *Asheville Citizen* about the rise in income tax cheating, "the social contract between the governed and the governors is in trouble."

Observations and questions

1) Pett seems to be undertaking an impossible writing task: To gauge Americans' vision of their country in a presidential election year. What Pett has done is to select a microcosm, Asheville, to represent the country. What does the word microcosm mean? What is its etymology? Can you think of any stories, perhaps in the *Wall Street Journal,* in which a person or a place is used to represent a larger reality? How do you go about selecting a microcosm? How do we know that Asheville is representative?

2) There are many voices in this piece. Who has Pett interviewed? Do they seem like the best sources for what Pett wants to know? Can you think of other potential sources in Asheville?

3) There are several references to Thomas Wolfe in this piece. Who was Wolfe? Don't confuse him with Tom Wolfe. Read *Look Homeward Angel* and see how Wolfe's vision of Asheville and America differs from Pett's.

4) In literary terms, Pett and the people of Asheville are evoking "the myth of the golden age," the idea that perfect happiness resides in the past. Look through the story for examples of how the golden age has crumbled in Asheville. Can you think of any other examples of this myth in literature, religions, popular culture or the memories of your parents or grandparents? Analyze this myth. Is it true that we are worse off than we once were? Do newspapers give that impression?

5) What is the effect of the words *ain't* and *'em*?

6) Returning to the playfulness of Pett's language, consider the phrases "gloom and doom" and "by the misty mysteries of the Blue Ridge." Some editors might consider this overwriting. Do you?

7) Pett tries to create both a sense of place and a sense of people. Consider the structure of this piece and analyze how Pett arranges his paragraphs about place and those about people.

8) Knowing the results of the election, do you think that Pett's analysis rings true? How did the city of Asheville go in the election? What does this say about the validity of the story? Aren't people always complaining about the quality of life?

A conversation with
Saul Pett

CLARK: We liked your Ed Koch story so much that we spent last week reading selections out loud to each other in the office. Where did you get the idea to do a piece on Koch?

PETT: In this case, it happened to be mine. I did not get a chance to do the presidential candidates last year, so I was looking for something, and there was our mayor. When you're in my business, the problem is finding people with real flavor and color to write about. Every year it's a greater problem because there are fewer and fewer of them. And he just seemed like a great subject.

What was the next step after you came up with the idea?

I started reading like crazy about him. Other things that had been done about him, some news stories, some previous profiles, until I got thoroughly familiar with him. Then I went down to City Hall and started to talk to people about him. People who worked for him. Others in politics. City Hall reporters. By the time I got to interview him, which I saved for last, I felt that I knew him.

Were people interested in talking about Koch?

Oh yes. Everybody's full of him. Everybody watches him or knows him. He's got that kind of personality. And everybody wants to talk about him. Usually the big problem is to get one good anecdote. I had them coming out of my ears here.

For every good one I had, there were three others that there was no room for.

It must have been a difficult job just to select the best ones.

The only real problem was one of selection, and throwing away. They all wanted to tumble out at once. This was a triumph of him, not me. The material was so good that you'd have to be a terrible writer to screw it up.

When you got the idea did you say to yourself: OK, I'm going to write about Ed Koch? Did you have a catalogue in your head of the people you wanted to talk to?

By now I approach it in some pattern. I wanted to talk to people who worked closely with him, see a lot of him. That's one type. Another type was people who had been around City Hall or New York politics a long time. They're terribly important to a story like this. They can compare him to Lindsay and others. And of course there's City Hall reporters.

Do you seek out people that you know are friends and adversaries?

Yes. It helps your perspective and your balance. Also it gives you a thing you need terribly. When you begin to hear a repetition of things, from both admirers and critics, a refrain, when both friend and foe agree that he's fresh, that he's candid, that he's tough, when you hear those refrains, you know that you're on the right track, that you've gotten something fairly solid.

Then you interviewed him?

Before I sat down for a formal interview, I travelled around the city with him for a couple of days and that was most useful. To see a man work, especially a colorful guy like this. We got in the car and went over to Brooklyn where they were dedicating a new shopping mall. Then we went to a new pier, and then we went to one of his "town hall" meetings. There were any number of little stops where he talked to people on the street. He loves to talk to people, even to be heckled by them. It's part of what he calls "street theater." And then I sat down with him in his office and we talked for a couple of hours at least.

How did you decide what to ask him?

I had a list of questions in mind. I usually do. I find that important. Even though there are spontaneous people involved, you should plan some questions. You're dealing with a busy guy, and you can lose him. Of course, with a guy like Koch, all you have to do is say hello. I had a big interview with Nixon in late 1972 in the Oval Office. This was just before Watergate blew up. With a president it's far more important to plan questions because you don't know how much time you're going to get. And it's hard to interrupt presidents. So you have to ask questions on different levels. First you have to interest him. Then you've got to find out what you want to find out. Well, in this case, Nixon was so full of himself — he had won an election very big, the whole world looked great to him. I asked him: How are you, and he took off. Every now and then I'd start to interrupt and cover a specific thing I had in mind. Then it occurred to me that I was getting a better story by just letting him talk. He was more self-revealing.

Do you have any interviewing techniques that you've developed over the years? Any tricks of the trade you can pass along?

I kind of plan the opening, either with a little humor, or something to relax them, or something that will interest them. I think the success of an interview depends on whether you interest the guy. You get him to where he feels like talking about himself. This sounds like a contradiction: The night before, I'll be sitting in a motel room, nervously trying to think of questions, and it makes for a more spontaneous interview.

In other words, if you're not struggling to think up questions, you've got an opportunity to be yourself.

I want it to be relaxed. Ideally the interview will come off like a conversation. There's another trick — it's so obvious — but it's a thing I had to learn: Relax, Charlie. Don't be a district attorney. Give the man time. Don't worry about a pause. If you ask him something and he says yes or no, and he pauses, you let him pause. He's thinking about something. You frequently get some awfully good things that way, letting the guy or woman talk. If you get an interview only on the basis of their quick and ready answers, you've got a kind of formal thing.

OK, you've got your research on Koch, notes, interviews with people who know him, you've followed him around, you've interviewed him. Now you've got a big job. Did you return to the office immediately after the interview and start writing?

I never go to the office immediately. My goodness. I stop at a bar and tell myself what a grand interviewer I am (laughs). As long as I've been in this business, I've learned there are different points in the story, levels of tension. When you start. When you've got all you're going to get before the interview with the principal. Then the interview is so important that you come out of it kind of tired. There's tension involved. And the next plateau is writing the damn thing.

I see in your work a playfulness in the use of

**language which is probably a mark of every
good writer. It's hard to learn how to create
images, metaphors and similes. They seem
to come naturally to you. The Koch piece is
filled with them.**

With a guy like Koch they come quickly, because his personality is so strong. But you just
sense when you need a metaphor. The nice thing
about a conversation like this is that you don't
know about the metaphors I threw away. Some of
them must have been horrors.

**Do you think you need to come up with some
bad ones in order to finally get to the good
ones?**

I think so. You know, even before I got to the interview with him, I thought I had the lead to the
story. It was one I never used. It was in my head, I
was in love with it, and it was wrong. The lead
was a short sentence: "We have by us a mayor, it
should happen to you." (Much laughter.) I loved
it. I couldn't shake it out of my head. But then
cooler heads prevailed as I got to the writing
stage. Would it be intelligible to the non-ethnics
around the country? I've got a closet full of leads I
haven't used. I've got phrases. I've always wanted to say: He's a man with an utterly resistible
personality. It was 20 years before I got to use
that — was it Jimmy Hoffa?

**How much editing do you get, Saul? Since
you're on Mt. Rushmore, do they keep their
hands off?**

My editor is a very good one. His name is Jack
Cappon. He's a superb student of writing. And
he's a good friend. I don't believe in turning in
anything that will need editing. I just think
that's a lazy way to write. It's less fun to write
that way. I like to have a sense of control over the
story. I don't think Jack's answer would be that I

require much editing. It's tightly written when it gets to him. When we get new editors here, I have a standard greeting for them: Now AP wants you to have imagination. Be bold. And above all, keep your goddam hands off my copy. (Laughs). And I'm not on Mt. Rushmore.

Do you write on a VDT?

I write on a typewriter. If I get a brilliant thought I write it on a cocktail napkin. I think I've left out a stage on the Koch story. Try to picture this. I'm back at the office now. I've got several notebooks full of stuff. I've got clips. I've got maybe portions of a book, or magazine pieces, taped interviews which I've transcribed. All that is done. There is my basic material. But it's all kind of in bunches. So then I sit down, and this is just dull donkey work, and I hate it, but I find it necessary, and I kind of outline my material. I don't outline the story because I don't know that yet. I'm outlining the material. I try to put it in piles. Here's stuff about Koch's wit. Here's stuff about his independence. Here's stuff about how he can be tough with minorities. Here's stuff about his background. All that exists in my notebooks scattered throughout. So the advantage of the outline is that I've got it on paper in logical segments. It's a lot of dull work. I spent two or three days at that.

At that point you're building up momentum, aren't you?

I'm getting more familiar with the material. So that when I'm ready to write, I don't have to pause and go fishing around in notebooks or in stacks of clips. By then I almost don't have to consult my notebooks. Then you sit down. And there's that little thing called a lead. I know that I don't spend as much time on leads as I used to. We make a mistake when we're younger. We feel compelled to hit a home run in the very first sentence. So we spend a lot of time staring at the typewriter. I'll settle for a quiet single, or even a long foul, anything that gets me started. When I talk to young writers, that's the most sensible advice I can give them. Perfect anecdotal leads are so rare. Even though Koch was full of good anecdotes, no one anecdote deserved to be the lead.

One of the few times one fell into my lap was some years ago when I went out to Beverly Hills to interview Dorothy Parker. She had just turned 70. She greeted me. It was 11 o'clock in the morning and she said, "Are you married, my dear?" I said Yes. She said "Well in that case, you won't mind zipping me up." Now I treasure that. It's one of the rare times in which a perfect anecdote for a lead was just handed to me (laughs).

Let's move to Asheville, North Carolina. How did you pick Asheville to do a piece on the national mood?

It was Jack Cappon's idea. We get our ideas just talking. He felt, and I agreed, that we ought to go out and try to pick up on the mood of the country in this election year. What I liked about Asheville, it is a beautiful spot, it has a history, it belonged to a state that was the first of the colonies to vote for independence, the next to the last to ratify the Constitution, and in the Civil War was one of the four border states which wavered over the question of secession. But I guess the biggest single reason was Thomas Wolfe. I could picture Asheville today against the Asheville he grew up in, and he was comparing his Ashevelle to his father's or grandfather's Asheville. So it was a wonderful way to start.

Now you've got a completely different sort of challenge than writing about a single person. You've got to conquer a whole town. How do you do that?

Well, you do it very imprecisely. It's unscientific. I don't attempt a poll or anything. I do talk to people. The man in the street. I also talk to people in a position to catch the mood of the community. Observers or people watchers. There are editors. Clergymen can frequently be damn good. A lawyer can be good. A real estate man can be good. The head of the Chamber of Commerce was good. When business people are pessimistic and critical about government, by God, you know there's a dark mood in the country. How do I know I'm going to be accurate about suggesting a general mood? Well, again, after a while you get a sameness. You begin to hear the same things over and over again. That's when you begin to get confident.

Did you do much research before getting to Asheville?

Oh, I read little "biographies" of Asheville. But mostly I reread Thomas Wolfe, whom I hadn't read in years. Reading *Look Homeward Angel* on the plane going down to Asheville, you get that picture of an America at another time of supreme confidence, where his father in the book is sounding off about Teddy Roosevelt and the Rough Riders. God, it was almost enough to weep to think that we once were that confident of ourselves and our purposes, and our ability. I just knew that would be in direct contrast to what I would find in Asheville today.

I've got a copy of a talk on writing that you gave some time ago. It begins "All sermons on writing that inhibit the writer are worse than the sins they're trying to correct."

That was given about 20 years ago to a meeting of AP bureau chiefs here. Our former boss thought that they would benefit from hearing a writer talk about writing. I was so nervous, I could hardly talk.

You say in that talk that "Before it's finished, good writing always involves a sense of discipline, but good writing begins in a sense of freedom, of elbow room, of space, of a challenge to grope and find the heart of the matter . . . ." We associate the wire services with the most traditional, the most conventional formula writing. And yet your writing, while it is disciplined, reflects the sense of freedom you're talking about. What would happen if somebody applied the Flesch test to the first sentence of your Koch story?

I'd flunk. Yes, I have strong feelings about silly things like the Flesch test. The length of a sentence should not be any kind of barometer unless it ends up unclear. The newspaper writer's first obligation is to be clear. And if he's unclear in a four-word sentence, he's committed the ultimate sin. Whether it's four words or forty words, it has to be clear. I find long sentences now and then a great help, a way of saying a certain thing with a kind of spirit, a momentum, a thrust, a flavor, a rhythm. I once set a course record by writing a lead that was 280 words long. It was a long sentence describing all the confusing things that had come up in a single day at a Republican convention. It ended up with the word "clear?" Of course, it wasn't clear. But then the day's activities weren't clear. The length of sentences and all those mechanical standards are kind of silly.

In your talk on writing you speak out against the notion that newspaper writers can't be "creative." You seem to be reacting against a tradition of journalism that ridicules the notion of creativity.

That was more true then than it is now. The traditional reporter and writer, and that included me, didn't want to have to think. He didn't want to have to find out how good or bad he was as a writer. It was much easier to blow it out of your left nostril. You know, a fast 20 minutes in the files, then you interview the guy for 20 minutes, and you learn nothing about him. Then you go across the street to the bar, telling yourself and whoever else might be interested that really if you had the time, you could have done a better story. Well, bullshit. Bullshit. We shouldn't have any more alibis. There was a line in a play once. I've forgotten the play, but I've never forgotten the line. The line was "Writing isn't hard, thinking is hard." Behind good writing is a basic logic, a basic common sense. What do I want to say about this fellow? What does it all add up to? What is the essence of this guy?

Was there some point in your life when you knew that you had an ability as a writer? That gift?

I didn't know it yesterday. Whatever you've done last week doesn't help this week. I'm in the middle of a big long involved piece about the federal bureaucracy, and I've never been so scared.

Richard Zahler
Deadline Writing

RICHARD ZAHLER has worked for the *Seattle Times* since 1973. He is now assistant city editor for special projects, a job that has both editing and writing responsibilities. He has served the *Times* as a general assignment reporter, City Hall reporter and copy editor. He has written "an ungodly number of column inches" on Washington's prisons and parole systems. Zahler is one of the leaders of the Seattle Times Writing Group, which works to improve the quality of writing on the newspaper. Now 33 years old, he received a degree in English from Whitman College and is quick to point out that Whitman is *not* Richard Nixon's alma mater. Before joining the *Times,* he worked for newspapers in Walla Walla and Spokane, and for the Associated Press. If any publishers are reading this, Zahler is trying to sell his first novel.

1,200 feet of St. Helens tossed to the wind

MAY 18, 1980

Eruption.

At 8:32 yesterday morning, Mount St. Helens ended seven weeks of nervous convulsions with an explosion brewed deep in the earth's primeval cauldron.

At least nine people were killed.

When the top of the volcano blew, upwards of 1,200 feet of mountaintop were pulverized. Instantly, the unimaginable tons of rock became tiny pebbles that fell as far away as Mount Rainier. The rock became gray sand in the streets of Yakima. It became a fine dust drifting like storm clouds in the sky above Spokane, then over Western Montana. Highways and airports were closed across the state.

The hot rock and ash also settled on the slopes of the mountain. A winter's mantle of ice and snow, already dingy from St. Helen's warm-up eruptions, melted into flowing death and destruction.

Within minutes of the eruption, snow, hot ash and superheated gases churned into mudflows dozens of feet thick. The mud started slowly down the mountain's broad flanks, gathered speed, then roared through timber and into the thin river valleys that normally carry burbling spring runoff.

The runoff yesterday was 12 feet high, a wall of water that gouged earth and timber from banks, spilling a mile-long logjam toward the Cowlitz and Columbia Rivers.

The water was so hot into the Toutle River that fish leaped from it to the banks, trying to escape.

The mud cascaded into Spirit Lake. The waters literally boiled, and the lake apparently was

The Seattle Times

given a new shape. One pilot said it seemed virtually to have ceased to exist.

On the mountain's south slope, the mud
rolled in the Swift Reservoir, the uppermost of
the three reservoirs on the Lewis River. There
was enough of it that the broad reservoir's level
rose 6 feet in 15 minutes.

Ahead of the crushing water and earth, minutes after the mountain's explosion, local police
went door-to-door in Toutle, telling residents to
leave or move to higher ground.

Most did. Some people in the area, apparently sight-seeing or hiking closer to the volcano,
didn't get the word.

Five bodies were found at Camp Baker, a
logging camp about 15 miles west of the mountain. Later, 1½ miles closer to the mountain, the
bodies of a man and a woman were found in their
car. Officials said they may have died from the
heat of mud and gas churning by. The bodies of
two campers were found nearer the mountain.

As volcanos have shaped the Northwest, so yesterday did Mount St. Helens leave its mark on the region: A black or gray cloud that hid the sun for thousands of square miles.

The ash filled the sky, and then it settled toward earth.

At noon in Yakima, it might as well have been midnight—"as dark as the darkest night you've ever seen," said a deputy sheriff.

Traffic stopped. Streetlights and neon signs flickered on.

The volcano began putting people into hospital emergency rooms a hundred miles away, with respiratory problems, with injuries suffered in accidents. Headlights could barely penetrate the black fog, and tires found little purchase on the slippery strata of ash on the highways.

There may be more from St. Helens. "It seems right now that the activity will go on for quite a while," a Geological Survey scientist said last night. "It could be hours or days."

A rage that filled the sky

MAY 25, 1980

Residents of the Pacific Northwest like to think they are blessed by nature and a benign deity.

There was no reason to think otherwise early, Sunday, May 18, 1980.

A bright sun rose in clear skies from the border of Eastern Washington to the Pacific Ocean beaches. In succession, its life-giving light bathed the young wheat stalks of the Palouse and the crops of the broad Columbia Basin. The sun shone on the blossoms and buds of Wenatchee's orchards, and hastened the ripening of another bountiful cherry crop in the Yakima Valley.

The sunrise glimmered off the snowy mountains of the Cascades, sparkled in a thousand crystalline lakes, caught the color of new wildflowers in the high meadows.

Rising above the Skamania County foothills, the sun illuminated the east slope of 9,677-foot Mount St. Helens. It did not reflect so brightly there, for the volcano in the past seven weeks had awakened from a century and a half of slumber. The snow on its slopes was dingy with ash.

Under the bright Sunday skies, barely broken here and there by high cirrus clouds, temperatures across Washington would climb into the 70s and 80s. Visibility was clear for dozens of miles.

With the region's long and damp winter clearly and finally behind them, thousands of Washington residents had set off for the weekend, driving across the state, camping, taking photographs. At home, others planned to spend the weekend working in their gardens, and others planned to do nothing at all but enjoy their weather and their land.

As the sun shone Sunday morning, Ron and Barbara Seibold and their two children were in the middle of one of the weekend outings they loved, watching deer, looking at the trees and flowers.

Not far away, Michael and Lu Moore were backpacking in beautiful high country north of Spirit Lake with their 4-year-old daughter, Bonnie Lu, and their baby, 3-month-old Terra.

To the north, in the little logging town of Morton, Pastor Thomas Slate had warmed up the Sunday School rooms in his United Methodist Church, made sure the church bulletins were in place, then returned to the parsonage for breakfast.

In Yakima, it was Police Chief Jack LaRue's day to manage the Yakima Valley Sportsman's Association's trapshooting club, and he loaded shotguns, ammunition, scorecards and other equipment into the trunk of his car.

In Spokane, for Mayor Ron Bair, there was levity in a relaxed Sunday schedule heavy with receptions and parties ending the annual Lilac Festival.

For each of them, and for thousands and thousands of other Washington residents, it was a million-dollar morning, full of spring and full of promise. Within hours—in some cases, minutes—the promises all were broken, and the day couldn't be traded for a few cents.

Mayor Bair's levity soured when he discovered sludge in the bottom of his beer cup, and when he drove through his city and found it as dusty and deserted as a ghost town.

Chief LaRue and his trapshooting friends didn't spend the day firing at clay pigeons in Yakima. They couldn't have seen the flying targets if they had wanted to.

In Morton, Pastor Slate rose to give his 11 o'clock sermon and, for the first time in his life, found every pew empty. Not a soul was in church.

For the Moore family of Castle Rock, the day became a nightmare that they didn't escape for more than 24 hours.

The four members of the Seibold family didn't escape the nightmare at all.

What mattered Sunday morning was not the clear sky and the bright sun. What mattered was at everyone's feet: the earth.

And it was not the early moments of a spring morning that made May 18 a day that will live in fearsome memory; it was a time span of millions of years.

For those millions of years, molten rock had been created deep within the earth by the stresses of primeval masses in collision. Gradually, over eons, the molten material worked its way toward the earth's surface. When the hot masses of rock and ash and gases breached the surface, they poured or exploded out. Over the millenia, mountains were built.

Of the Pacific Northwest's many volcanoes, Mount St. Helens was regarded widely as the most beautiful. Its graceful slopes, symmetrical and smooth, are a consequence of the mountain's relative youth. The peak's visible portions have existed for perhaps only 2,500 years, not enough time for glaciers to carve her features into irregularity.

St. Helens' youthfulness and relatively recent history of activity, including a major eruption 123 years ago, caused scientists to believe it was among the likeliest anywhere to erupt in this century.

Events of March, 1980, began to prove them right.

On March 20, the mountain began to rumble. For the next week its tremors sent the needles of seismographs in Seattle dancing across scientists' charts.

On March 27, the mountain blew out a new crater on its summit. Steam and ash rose 7,000 feet in the air. Mount St. Helens became a scientific attraction and a news celebrity overnight. Geologists and reporters flew in from around the country.

For weeks, the steam ventings and seismic rumblings continued. But then, as with any star who doesn't work up a new act periodically, Mount St. Helens' glimmer of celebrity waned. The journalists went home. The loggers who had evacuated the forests at the mountain's base gradually returned to work.

The fear and mystery of the first eruption diminished. Adventurers and photographers evaded sheriff's patrols to ascend the mountain and peer into the crater. Summer-home owners demanded to be allowed past roadblocks to visit their property. The Skamania County sheriff complained that maps had been printed detailing just how sightseers could circumvent his roadblocks.

Instead of a source of worry, Mount St. Helens became for many a source of jokes, an inspiration to entrepreneurs who funneled volcanic ash into plastic bags and peddled them as souvenirs.

But the scientists didn't stop worrying.

Late in April they reported that a massive area on the mountain's northeast face had started steadily bulging out. Molten material was climbing inside the volcano. Pressure built. Trying to accommodate that force, the mountain stretched and reshaped itself.

In the weeks after the first eruption, scientists watched the volcano from close at hand at Timberline camp, an outpost about 4,500 feet up Mount St. Helens' northeast slope, 4 miles from Spirit Lake.

One of them, David Johnston of the Geological Survey, went closer than anyone—into the crater.

Johnston respected the volcano. He was nearly trapped on Alaska's Mount St. Augustine when it erupted in January, 1976. Before descending into Mount St. Helens' crater to retrieve water samples in April, he stood on the crater rim for two hours watching avalanche patterns inside, planning his route.

But though Johnston respected the mountain, and knew as well as anyone the potential fury building inside, he could not take himself far from the volcano.

As the worrisome bulge grew on the mountain's north side, the geologists abandoned their Timberline camp. They believed the threat of slides from the mountain was growing, and the camp was too close.

A new camp was established, Coldwater II, on a ridge north of the Toutle River Valley, 5 miles from the volcano's summit. Johnston lived there in a mobile home, watching the mountain, periodically radioing other scientists in Vancouver.

Saturday night, May 17, Johnston called in that nothing was happening. Sunday morning, the red radio-telephone carried his voice again to Forest Service headquarters. Still nothing to report.

A few minutes later, Johnston radioed his last call:

"Vancouver! Vancouver! This is it!

"Vancouver! Vancouver! Is the transmitter still working?!"

The message wasn't heard in Vancouver.

A ham-radio operator picked up the call.

It was 8:32 a.m.

The mountain was exploding.

Johnston's outpost was directly in the path of what geologists later said was a completely unexpected, almost unprecedented horizontal explosion of superheated gas and debris from the mountain, a planetary cannon blast.

The concussion of that explosion leveled tall evergreens for miles, stripped them of their branches, left them stacked and aligned on the ground like cordwood.

Where there had been a bulge on the mountain, there grew a crater as millions of tons of rock and ice—the top 2,000 feet or more of Mount

St. Helens—was demolished.

The boulders and rocks sprayed to the north. The part of the mountaintop that was pulverized into pebbles and dust rose billowing 9 or 10 miles into the air, first rolling like the black smoke of an oil fire, then broadening in a frightening mushroom cap as the gases and ash poured higher.

Far above the mountain, the ash was caught by southwesterly winds, to become disaster in another form as it blew north and east, darkening the Sunday sky over thousands of square miles. The ash landed in the orchards and bowed the fragile wheat stalks of Washington's farming heartland. It stranded thousands of people.

At the mountain itself the explosion created what scientists said would be the volcano's most destructive force if it blew—a "pyroclastic flow," a descending wall of hot gas and water and ashen mud. It roared off the mountain, obliterating and burying whatever was standing in its path, slamming into the once-pristine waters of Spirit Lake.

The hot mud and gas plunged into the forks of the Toutle River, gouging out wider valleys. Displaced by the mud, water in the river rose instantly, creating its own wall of destruction. Timber, roads, bridges and cabins were swept from the map. Trees torn from the banks tumbled into a mile-long logjam that crashed toward the Cowlitz and Columbia Rivers.

The water-borne mud followed. The Cowlitz turned to chocolate milk. As the mud settled out it created the foundation for what could become future floods. The mud raised the Cowlitz riverbed by 15 feet at Castle Rock, just below the outflow of the Toutle; downstream at Longview, the mud raised the riverbed by 8 feet.

Not all of it stopped there. Enough mud and debris flowed from the Cowlitz into the Columbia River to fill in its ship channel for two miles.

At week's end, geologist David Johnston was listed among the many missing after Mount St. Helens' eruption. A helicopter pilot who flew over Coldwater II reported that it was 4 to 5 feet deep in ash, littered with tree fragments and boulders and chunks of ice several feet in diameter.

A few miles north of Johnston's Coldwater II camp was Coldwater I, a photo observatory. Stationed there was Reid Blackburn, a Vancouver *Columbian* photographer under contract to the Geological Survey and National Geographic Society. He was not heard from Sunday morning. Pilots said Coldwater I was devastated in the volcano's first explosion. Blackburn's body was found four days later.

Also unheard from was Bob Kasewater of Portland, owner of a cabin on the shore of Spirit Lake, a geologist who worked for General Electric and one of two persons with permission to be at the lake. He was taking pictures of the mountain for future study, and had rigged up a battery-operated seismograph. With him on Saturday, when a reporter visited, was a scientist-friend from General Electric, Bev Wetherald. They showed off the equipment and their view of the mountain from the porch of the cabin. On Sunday morning, the cabin ceased to exist.

The other property owner with permission to be at the lake was Harry Truman, the 83-year-old lodge owner who became a folk hero by virtue of his stubborn refusal to leave his home of 54 years. The mud and rock and gas flowed over the shore and into Spirit Lake, leaving no sign of Harry Truman, his lodge, his 16 cats or his player piano.

Pastor Thomas Slate's mind may have been on Heaven early Sunday morning. His thoughts decidedly were on the heavens by late Sunday morning.

Mount St. Helen's first explosion spewed dark clouds of ash and mud in a mighty roar to the north.

In the logging town of Morton, 30 miles away, a parishioner called Mr. Slate at the

United Methodist Church and told him to look to the south. The minister did and saw the dark volcanic cloud looming above the foothills.

"It was, of course, glowing with sunshine on the east face of the cloud. Underneath there were flashes of lightning. There was a good deal of lightning. I didn't hear the sound of the eruption, but I heard thunder rolling in the distance as the lightning crackled."

Observing that display, Mr. Slate didn't forget practical matters. From newspaper accounts, he knew he should expect ash fallout from the volcano. He carried a tank-type vacuum cleaner to the vestibule of his church to help clean any members of the congregation who might arrive for services.

The sky over Morton turned black by 9:30 a.m. Seven people showed up for Sunday school. Half an hour later, they walked outside into a town that Mr. Slate remembers being "as dark as midnight on a moonless night."

Mud rained from the sky in balls the size of pencil erasers. It coated everything. Ash drifted in, and five people went to the hospital with breathing problems.

At 11 o'clock, no one from Mr. Slate's 160-member congregation had arrived for the regular worship service.

"I played the organ and sang some hymns by myself and when, at 11:20, no one had arrived, I simply made a prayer and closed the church up, closing all the doors and sealing it as tight as I could." Then he sealed up the Sunday School rooms, and returned to the parsonage and sealed it up.

By 12:15 p.m. the sky began to lighten again.

That evening the police called and asked Mr. Slate to put up stranded travelers. Nine of them, in two families, joined him at the parsonage, and he retrieved the vacuum cleaner from the church so they could clean the ash off themselves.

By week's end, Thursday and Friday, the

heavens sent rain. The dust settled. Some of the mud washed away.

The people of Morton took the eruption well, Mr. Slate said. There seemed to be no fears of disaster.

"On the contrary, the people I've been in contact with have reminded me of the promises of God to watch over us and have also reminded me that we don't have any real security in this world and we should be prepared under all circumstances for such things as the shaking of the earth and pouring out of these destructive energies.

"And, of course, I have agreed with them."

For today's sermon Mr. Slate said he will draw from the Bible's 12th Chapter of Hebrews, a vision of contrasts between the volcanic fury of Mount Sinai and the love represented by Mount Zion.

In part, the chapter reads:

"For ye are not come unto the mount that might be touched and that burned with fire, nor unto blackness and darkness and tempest ... But ye are come unto Mount Zion, and unto the city of the living God, the heavenly Jerusalem, and to an innumerable company of angels."

Residents of the Yakima Valley who looked west toward the Cascade Mountains might well have been forgiven if a Biblical analogy came to mind. Mount St. Helens was about to deliver a plague of dust on all their houses.

Sheriff's Sgt. Larry Gamache learned at 9:18 a.m. that the mountain had erupted. Twenty minutes later, a huge black cloud crested the mountains. "It was kind of unbelievable. It gradually went from a bright sunlight to gray, to muddy brown, to black."

By noon Sunday, on a day that began with at least 50 miles of visibility in any direction, Yakima was "as dark as the darkest night you've ever seen," Gamache said. It stayed that way for nearly 36 hours.

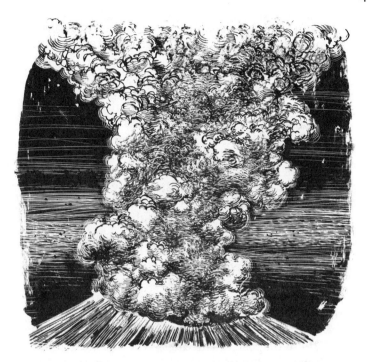

As the volcanic ash closed in, traffic stopped in the streets. Sheriff's patrolmen were ordered to stop in their cars, do nothing, wait for instructions.

Police Chief Jack LaRue never made it to the regular Sunday trapshoot practice at the Yakima Valley Sportsman's Association club. At first it looked like rain.

"I noticed an obviously very black cloud forming to the west and thought, wow, we're going to get a rainstorm. And pretty soon I began to hear the hiss on the rooftops and found that the rain was pretty dry. In fact, it was downright stony."

LaRue went to work. He found that people were busy, but said there seemed to be no real emergencies. Officers were assigned to 12-hour shifts and watch commanders drifted in to help. After six hours, the chief decided it would be all right to knock off for the day, go home and have dinner.

"I think the people of the community responded very well under the circumstances," he said.

As the day and week progressed, ash that was the size of BB shot on Sunday morning gradually turned to finer stuff that sifted through clothing, through paper breathing masks, through the cracks around doors and windows.

By late in the week there still was fine ash in Yakima's air, but it was hard to tell whether it was coming from the sky or simply being lifted from the streets, billowing with each slowly passing car or truck. As Yakima gradually started going about business again, the ash continued to rise underfoot from sidewalks where it lay strewn inches deep.

A bank in the city posted a plea outside: "For security reasons, please remove masks before entering."

Some organization gradually was brought to efforts to dispose of the dust. Wet ash turned out to have the general properties of wet concrete, and residents were told not to hose down the sidewalks and streets, for fear of fouling storm-drainage systems. Instead, they were asked to scoop the ash into containers and carry it to landfills.

Yakima city workers used snowplows to push the stuff into piles to be loaded onto dump trucks. After roads opened, the cities of Seattle and Portland, spared by the winds, sent some of their equipment to help.

Like many Eastern Washington cities, Yakima found itself with stranded travelers when the curtain of ash dropped Sunday. The Red Cross quickly opened five emergency shelters, and the town played host to about 350 extra persons the first night.

By Monday the highway south to Goldendale was passable and the bold slowly headed out. In Goldendale, outside the heavy ash-drift, motorists paused and lined up at service stations for oil changes and new air filters.

By Wednesday afternoon, the first direct highway link to Western Washington was re-opened over White Pass.

More than 5,000 travelers were stranded at one time in Eastern Washington, and they straggled out for days after ash choked, then closed, virtually every major highway east of the mountains.

But for more than 100 near-victims of the Mount St. Helens' devastation in Cowlitz and Skamania Counties, the people who mattered most got out just in time.

People like Mark Edelbrock.

Edelbrock is a Seattle fire fighter. On week-ends and during longer exercises, he is tactical operations commander for the helicopter attack troop of the 116th Armored Cavalry regiment, based at Fort Lewis.

With other pilots and crew members, he was in Yakima Saturday preparing for two weeks of annual maneuvers.

Before the thickening ash made flying impossible Saturday, most of the helicopters got out. They proved crucial in the difficult mission of finding the people who somehow had survived the hot gases, swirling ash and churning mud and water of eruption.

It may never be certain just how many hikers and campers and sightseers had found their way into the restricted forest near the mountain Sunday. Official lists of the missing grew and shrank in the days after the eruption—a handful of persons at first, then more than 100, down again to less than 70, then back up by a few more persons unaccounted for.

Some of those, such as geologists and government employees, were around the mountain for official reasons. There were loggers who had permission to work close to the mountain. And there were sightseers who had either purposely skirted roadblocks or found their way in through a web of Forest Service and logging roads simply too extensive to be patrolled effectively.

"People went over, under, through and around, every time we tried to restrict access to what we believed to be dangerous areas," said Sheriff William Closner of Skamania County. "There were even maps sold showing how to get around our blockades on the mountain. It would have taken the U.S. Army to contain those people."

The Army and the National Guard weren't there to keep anybody out before the eruption. But, by their estimates, their helicopters brought more than 150 survivors out afterwards, most of them on Sunday as steam and ash still swirled thickly in the devastated landscape north of the mountain.

For the pilots, the hours were long and dangerous. There was difficulty seeing. Often, the aircraft could not land because of the thick ash their rotors would send boiling up around them.

The chopper crews persevered. They saw wrecked cars in the debris of toppled timber and ravaging mud. They dropped for a look. Sometimes they could see lifeless bodies below, and they made a note of the location with map coordinates. The dead would have to wait.

Sometimes they could see footprints in the thick ash, leading away from the cars. Those map coordinates were noted as well. If no one was seen alive, helicopters would check again later, or the next day.

Sometimes there were incidents that rekindled hope in pilots frustrated by the gray lifelessness that seemed to stretch endlessly below them in the shattered hills.

Tuesday night, preparing at 9 p.m. to return his Huey helicopter to the Army's Gray Field near Tacoma, Edelbrock decided to make one more pass over the Toutle River. Near the "Y" where the river's North and South Forks join, he noticed flashing lights.

When Edelbrock and his three crew members investigated, they found a 65-year-old man with his dog. The helicopter landed and picked them up. The man had gone up the river to try to retrieve belongings, then was stranded by rising water. He had turned on the flashers of his car.

Other rescues were accomplished in this alien inferno.

When the volcano erupted, Michael and Lu Moore of Castle Rock, with a 4-year old daughter, Bonnie Lu and an infant, 3-month-old Terra, were backpacking along the Green River Trail, more than a dozen miles and two high ridges northwest of Mount St. Helens. The explosion kept them from reaching their car. The trails became unrecognizable under the fallen trees and ash.

The Moores made camp again Sunday night. At noon Monday, a helicopter appeared, but was unable to land because of the dangerous dust. Eventually crewmen were lowered, and they led the family to a landing zone.

Another family of four was not so fortunate.

Ron Seibold and his wife, Barbara, loved the Mount St. Helens area. With their children, Michelle, 9, and Kevin, 7, they drove there often on weekends from their home in Olympia, where he worked for the state Department of Transportation and she worked as a teacher's aide at Olympia High School.

On Sunday they apparently were going to Fawn Lake, about 10 miles northwest of the peak. By shortly after 8:30 a.m. their car had reached Camp Baker, about 15 miles west of the mountain. They got no farther.

The Seibold family, apparently killed by the heat and gas exploding through the Toutle Valley, were among the first identified victims of the eruption.

They and others who were killed around Mount St. Helens are believed to be the first recorded fatalities of a volcanic eruption in the contiguous 48 states.

Eastern Washington did not have life-and-

death dramas. It just had dust and ash.

The known casualties were cars, abandoned because it was impossible to see the roads or because they choked up and refused to run. The stranded travelers were homeless only temporarily, but there were thousands of them, and at times they taxed the ingenuity of the small towns that accepted them.

In Ritzville, the Rev. Rea Thompson and his Methodist congregation were singing the closing hymn when the sanctuary darkened. Somebody flipped on the lights. Then they moved out into the strangely cool air and ooh-ed and ahh-ed at the black cloud overhead.

"I lived in Texas for a while, and it looked a lot like a tornado cloud—black and billowing. It took a while to register what it was."

By 2 p.m., the town was in darkness. There was a light rain of ash as Rea and Judy Thompson walked to a meeting at the neighboring Lutheran Church. The ashfall grew heavier and they ran back home, arriving "coated with the stuff."

Meanwhile, dozens of motorists, blinded by the darkness and ashfall, engines clogged, already had straggled off I-90 and into the isolated town. Quickly Ritzville's four motels filled up. Police started referring people to the churches.

Five college students from Cheney were the first to arrive on Mr. Thompson's doorstep. They heard the first eruption reports, set out to see for themselves and drove directly into the path of the ash cloud.

A motel operator phoned and asked if the pastor could accommodate a family of four more.

Folks would be hungry, Mr. Thompson figured, so he hustled off to buy pancake flour and syrup. "When I got back, there were 30 to 40 people in the house." He went back for more flour, and came home to find 60 people.

That night, Mr. Thompson counted 127 people sleeping in his house and church.

They were from as near as Spokane and Chelan, as far as Minnesota and Alaska. They were sightseers returning from the Lilac Festival and air show in Spokane, cowboys from a calf-roping competition in Ritzville, two honeymooners, a Kirkland couple, traveling businessmen, a California woman driving a motor home, two parade-float drivers dressed in pink frilled shirts and tuxedoes . . . . By the end of the day, up to 2,000 ash-coated freeway travelers had converged on the little farm town. And Ritzville accommodated the lot—in guest rooms and living rooms, on church pews and gymnasium floors.

Stella Hilzer, manager of the local Eagles Club, hosted 21—all Eagles who had driven to Ritzville for a club meeting. Many others took 10 or more unexpected guests. "The people just kept coming and we kept taking them in," Mrs. Hilzer said.

Lynn Lupfer, the grade-school principal, figures he had close to 500 people sleeping in two school gymnasiums.

They included several rough-edged workers in a traveling "carnival"—they camped amid theater sets on the school stage, then set out to tour the town bars. By Monday, there was trouble—some drinking and fisticuffs, Lupfer said.

Ritzville took care of that problem. The mayor closed the bars, and prohibited any more liquor sales.

Back at the Methodist Church, Mr. Thompson watched leaders emerge among the stranded travelers. "It was amazing. People just recognized what was needed and took over." They ran off to the store, and signed up to cook, wash dishes, entertain children and sweep away the omnipresent volcanic ash.

The comings and goings of scores of people made the control of the gray dust a momentous task. At the school gymnasium, Lupfer set up a chain of vacuum cleaners leading straight to the showers.

But the 127 people at the Methodist Church were sharing one shower — the Thompsons'.

So it was showers "by appointment only."

On Monday night, Ritzville stores ran out of spaghetti and hamburger. Supplies of other foodstuffs soon were in short supply.

By Tuesday—more than 48 hours after the eruption—Mr. Thompson began seeing subtle signs of cabin fever.

"People were hearing news reports. Seattle didn't have any of the stuff and Spokane didn't seem too bad. People were wondering if the rest of the world had forgotten us."

Telephone lines remained jammed. People couldn't get through to their families or employers.

They were confused and frustrated by mixed conflicting advice from the authorities. They first were told to breathe through a wet rag, then advised a dry rag was better, then told again to use a wet one. Do you sweep or wash the stuff away? Is it safe to drive or not?

Folks at the Methodist Church found ways to laugh at their predicament. They sang their own version of a popular folk song—"This ash is your ash/ This ash is my ash." They concocted volcanic puns—"We bit the dust" and "Washington, the Evergray State."

They mixed ash and water to sculpt miniature volcanoes topped with red chalk.

"You probably won't believe this, but morale was really high most of the time," Mr. Thompson said. "There's even talk of a reunion."

By midday Thursday, the last of the Thompsons' guests were gone. A dozen ash-clogged automobiles remained in the driveway, much more secure than the hundreds of abandoned cars which littered the cross-state freeway.

One resident derived some consolation from the fact that "most all the State Patrol cars are blowed up."

The Thompsons, Lupfers, Hilzers and other Ritzville residents turned to digging themselves out from under 4 inches of ash.

"It's a real mess," Mrs. Hilzer laughed.

"There's no lawn and no garden. Just one darn, yellow dandelion sticking up out of the gray— right in the middle of the yard."

Mayor Ron Bair of Spokane was wearing black slacks, a black tie and a lilac-colored sports jacket Sunday morning. The city's annual Lilac Festival was in its last day and his schedule was full:

A festival brunch as part of Aerospace Day at Fairchild Air Force Base . . . an afternoon kegger at the home of a local newspaper columnist . . . then a cocktail party hosted by former Mayor Neal Fosseen . . . finally, dinner with two guests from Spokane's sister city in Japan.

He learned about the eruption during brunch, but it would be hours before the enormity of the effect on the city would become apparent. When Col. John Shaud announced to the diners that Mount St. Helens had erupted, they joked that the Air Force planned it as a rousing finale to the Lilac Festival. Bair and everyone else never thought anything about ash fallout.

The western sky had turned dark blue by the time Bair and his wife, escorted by an officer, were looking at an SR-71 spy plane, brought in to be the key exhibit in the show. The delicate plane would be moved indoors if ash were detected, an officer said. At just that moment Bair's lips felt coated. He told his wife he felt like he was in a dusty room. It must have been a premonition. Not until seven hours later, with the sunny skies turned pitch dark, would he see his black tie turn gray with ash.

Driving back to town, Bair was slightly irritated as he and his wife listened to radio reports about the ashfall and darkness in Yakima. The former television newsman wished reporters wouldn't exaggerate so. Total darkness in Yakima? People might panic hearing reports like that.

Still the sky was looking weird, a description

he used repeatedly, so he decided to take a look from the panoramic viewpoint of the city's High Drive. The sky still looked dark blue with a gray haze, like a storm cloud. It looked like it would veer toward the north end of the city, like many thunderstorms do.

Bair chatted on High Drive for half an hour with the city health officer and a former city councilman, who happened to be there taking a look, too. The sky kept getting darker and Bair drove off to another viewpoint, listening, but not quite believing the radio news reports. There, for the first time, he saw a definite line in the sky "like something out of a crazy science-fiction movie." The color had changed from blue to black, he said to his wife in surprise.

The first ash began falling about 2 p.m. when they stopped at a store before heading home to get ready for the parties and dinner. By 3 p.m., it was like midnight outside. About that time, he looked skyward when he went to get the car from the garage. He mentioned that it felt like dust in his eyes. The falling ash looked like snow in the headlights when he backed his car from the garage. He thought what was happening was interesting.

The seven-minute drive to the columnist's house took 30 minutes. He and his wife joked about Pompeii as they crept along in the blowing dust. He parked across the street from the party and they ran across the street as if to avoid getting wet. Shock registered for the first time when he looked at his tie. It was white.

He accepted a beer drawn from a keg in the backyard, then went upstairs with a reporter— the room was full of them—to give his reactions to the eerie events unfolding. He sipped and talked in David Brinkley-cadences. He was about to take his last swallow of beer. "My God, I'm drinking mud," he said. The bottom of the glass was a gray beer-ash sludge.

He thought about what he, as mayor, ought to do. The storm was an act of God and state and county governments would take care of closing roads, so there didn't seem much he could do. He checked in with his office. Everything was under control; just stand by, he was told.

The sky had begun to brighten after about 1½ hours of darkness. Mostly a nuisance, he thought. He gathered up his wife and headed for the cocktail party downtown. He wasn't prepared for what he was about to see.

No one was in the business district. "It was like the city was empty for 100 years and had been gathering dust."

He was the cocktail party's only guest. The former mayor told him that all festival events were canceled.

Suddenly, Bair began to sense something frightening was going on, something over which he and everyone else had no control.

He went back to his car, turned on the air conditioner and began driving through the empty city with his wife, still listening to radio reports. He wanted to absorb what was happening.

At 11:30 he took his wife home and called his office for an update. Everything was shut down. The sheriff had declared a state of emergency. Bair went to bed.

It was the last real sleep he was to get for days.

His was the only car on the street when he went to the mayor's office on Monday. He tried to keep buses running, but gave up in the afternoon when one bus engine burned out and 20 other buses were disabled by ash. On Tuesday, police reported that the number of family fights was much higher than usual. Crime was down, though, except for the one young burglar who was caught when police followed his tracks through the ash.

Bair worried about whether the city's six-day supply of food would run out and told the governor the only help he might need would be to restock grocery shelves if the emergency continued.

He asked people to wash down the streets in front of their homes and found neighborhoods were challenging neighborhoods over radio shows to see who would have the cleanest streets. He thought the people's response was great.

He wonders about what strange effects may be revealed in the days and weeks ahead. For instance masses of insects died in the ashfall. What's that going to do to the birds that depend on them for food? And why are there so few birds around?

That's just curiosity, though, compared to his worries about the microscopic particles of jagged glass that his air-pollution experts tell him are slowly falling from the sky. He wonders if cities like Denver, outside the ash zone, have any idea of what might be raining on them unseen.

Bair has ordered everyone to wear face masks, and President Carter promised 2 million would be delivered free to Eastern Washington.

The mayor is particularly worried about kids breathing the stuff, and he's angry at parents who let their children out without protection. He's about to the point where he'll have police arrest people outside without the masks. He's already ordered city employees to wear them or be fired. Period. Don't bother to show up for work again if you're caught without a mask on, he told them.

Thursday night he was home for the first real rest since Monday.

The upper Toutle Valley lay devastated under mud and fallen timber. The lower valley remained threatened by floods.

But two guys from out of town were feeling pretty smug in Toutle Tuesday morning. They'd outsmarted the police at the roadblock and had driven right up to the mudslide. They hadn't forgotten to bring along a supply of beer.

"Wanna interview me? I'll be the next Harry

Truman," one proclaimed, punctuating his re-
mark with the foamy pop of a 12-ounce can.

A couple of hundred yards away, Bill Cartner was taking things a bit more seriously, load-
ing his family's belongings in his flatbed truck.

Mount St. Helens already had buried his job
and trapped his hogs. And now, deputies warned,
it might be ready to take another shot at his
house.

"I've been here 20 years," Cartner said. "Sure
hate to see anything happen to it."

Much of Toutle had been evacuated Sunday
in the initial surge of mud and debris into the
river. Then came word that water in Spirit Lake
was mounting behind a massive mudflow that
might give way at any time. Rumors of a 200-foot
wall of water kept Toutle under the shadow of
doom for most of the week. Although alarm about
the situation lessened later in the week, the reports did serious damage to the nerves and com-
posure of residents.

"We don't know what's coming next," said Cartner's wife, Judy. While her daughter, Melissa, 14, fed the chickens, Mrs. Cartner tried to decide what to take along as the family evacuated.

Finally, truck loaded, they headed to Longview to stay at the home of a nephew.

During the daytime, until Wednesday night, Toutle residents were allowed back in for short visits to pick up essentials. At regular intervals, a patrol car would come by to discourage dallying.

It didn't take long for Toutle to become a ghost town. Stores and gas stations were closed and quiet.

In Sunday's initial evacuation, Cartner helped alert local residents, using a loudspeaker attached to the outside of his truck.

"We were about the last ones out," said Judy, secretary of a local citizens' band radio club.

Cartner, a timber-faller, had worked at Weyerhaeuser's Camp Baker, which virtually was destroyed by the eruption. He said he didn't know whether the company would have work for him at another location.

The mudslide had cut off a road between Cartner's home and the piece of property where he keeps his four hogs. Judy tried to haul feed to them and found the route impassable.

Cartner didn't protest the evacuation, as some did. Nor did he argue, complain, and insult the deputies, as some did. He just said he hoped he could go back soon.

"What we like about it here," Cartner said, "is it's always been a quiet town up until now."

As much as they might hope, their Toutle Valley home will not be the same for Bill and Judy Cartner. What it will be for them is uncertain, as so much has been uncertain in the week since Mount St. Helens erupted, and as so much will remain.

It is the kind of uncertainty that, every afternoon last week, prompted Denice Krawl, when she finished her bakery job in Longview, to drive her daughter across the bridge to Rainier, Ore., to spend the night in the car, though her home outside Kelso was undamaged.

In Eastern Washington, it is the kind of uncertainty that cannot envision weeks and months of living in ash. Calls mounted through the week to Spokane Crisis Services. For the time being, people are finding ways of dealing with the ash, said the coordinator, Tom Peters; what they are having trouble with is the anxiety it creates.

In Cowlitz and Skamania Counties, there is economic uncertainty. The timber industry supports hundreds of jobs, and the industry is damaged. A Weyerhaeuser Co. vice president Jack Wolff, said the company can find logs for its Longview mill elsewhere, but faces unknown difficulties with its Toutle Valley timber operation.

Even if those difficulties are surmountable, the loggers and their families may be uncertain about the forests around the mountain as the volcano continues to spit steam and ash.

Scientists had guessed the mountain would give some warning of a major eruption. It didn't. Had the explosion not come on a Sunday, the casualty toll likely would have been higher. "If it had been a weekday, our husbands and fathers would be dead," said Rickey Foster of Silver Lake.

There is economic uncertainty in Eastern Washington.

Harvey Olander retired from his job as a geologist a year ago and settled with his wife on a 40-acre apple orchard near Yakima. Now his apple trees carry a lesson in geology, and Olander just shakes his head and shakes the dust from the trees.

"I've lived through about every possible natural disaster you can imagine. I've been through earthquakes in Colombia . . . typhoons in the South Pacific . . . floods like you wouldn't believe in Malaysia.

"But I've never seen anything like this.

You'd have to be clairvoyant to know what this will really do the crops."

Field crops could suffer major losses, particularly the thousands of acres of wheat bent under the weight of ash, state agriculture officials say.

There is concern in Longview and Kelso about the Cowlitz River. With its riverbed built up by dense volcanic mud, the river's banks and dikes may turn out to be several crucial feet too low for traditional runoff.

The Columbia River is a worry. While ocean-going ships had begun moving through the clogged channel of the river by the end of the week, the channel will not be restored to its original width and depth until September 30, according to the Army Corps of Engineers, which estimates that the job of dredging the channel will cost about $25 million. The Port of Portland estimated that it was losing at least $500,000 a day while the channel was plugged.

And, of course, there is uncertainty about the mountain.

Until two months ago, in the memory of every living person, Mount St. Helens, shimmering across Spirit Lake, stood as a ready symbol of benign and beautiful nature in the Pacific Northwest.

The mountain never will symbolize that again to those who have seen the destruction that has been wrought, or to the thousands whose lives have been wrenched in the days since that bright, peaceful and deceptive Sunday morning of May 18, 1980.

Observations and questions

1) This is a story about an awesome natural phenomenon. In the lead to his May 25 piece Zahler says that "Residents of the Pacific Northwest like to think they are blessed by nature and a benign deity." He also reminds his readers that "the volcano in the past seven weeks had awakened from a century and a half of slumber." In both cases he personifies nature, an archetypal human impulse which even pervades our television commercials ("You can't fool Mother Nature"). It's also a poetic impulse and a primitive religious one (in the 1951 movie *Bird of Paradise* a virginal Debra Paget jumps into a volcano to appease an angry island god). Look carefully at the way the forces of nature are characterized and personified. To what extent does this contribute to our understanding of what happened to the people of Washington on the day of the eruption?

2) Zahler's lead has a magazine quality. It serves as a way of introducing the story, sets a mood, foreshadows events, and presents important characters. Compare it to the lead reprinted below in which Steve Lovelady of the *Philadelphia Inquirer* introduces a long narrative on the events of Three Mile Island:

4:07 a.m., March 2, 1979.

Two pumps fail. Nine seconds later, 69 boron rods smash down into the hot core of unit two, a nuclear reactor on Three Mile Island. The rods work. Fission in the reactor stops.

But it is already too late.

What will become America's worst commercial nuclear disaster has begun.

Unit two at Three Mile Island is out of control. And no one knows. No one will know, for hours.

During the next six days, America—and the world—will watch in terror and dismay as the best minds available try to prevent apocalypse. They will see scientists grappling with events they had never anticipated; federal officials frozen by indecision for days; a small, previously obscure utility company haplessly repeating like a broken record that everything is all right; and a state government struggling fruitlessly to find out what is going on and what is to be done.

What they will not see are the details behind these reactions—details more harrowing even than the general impression: Nuclear workers playing Frisbee outside a plant gate because they were locked out but not warned of the radiation beaming from the plant's walls; federal officials meeting 55 hours after the accident to be briefed, and learning to their dismay that the experts could not describe what was going on; company officials meeting behind closed doors eight days after the accident to discuss not how to get the facts out but how to keep the facts hidden; broken valves fastened together with sealing compound; a state official trying for two days to get briefed by federal officials and when he finally heard from them, being so shocked by what they had to say that he buried his head in his hands and cried: "Oh, my God." There were also instances when men in charge, under tremendous pressure, rose to the moment.

At 7 a.m. Wednesday, a technician in the Three Mile Island control room realized that radiation was seeping from the complex. He reached for a phone and called—not his bosses but the state civil defense office and the federal Nuclear Regulatory Commission.

Thus, men responsible for the public interest learned of the problem before men responsible for the company's bottom line were informed.

But such moments were rare.

The story from the outside was hair-raising enough to a nation confronted by the unknown.

The story from the inside is more alarming yet.

Twenty-eight *Inquirer* reporters over the last 10 days have tracked down hundreds of those involved—plant-workers, scientists, government and utility officials, and residents—to discover the true dimensions of the crisis at Three Mile Island.

Here is their account . . . .

3) In the interview with Zahler, his lead is described as having Micheneresque qualities. Read the beginnings of several James Michener novels and see if you agree.

4) The time element is a key to the structure of this long piece. Using the moment of eruption as a focal point, draw a diagram that charts the chronology. How does Zahler use time to create suspense and maintain interest?

5) This news event is so big, so astonishing in magnitude, that it tests the writer's ability at every turn. Zahler seems to combine two approaches. One is of grandeur and breadth, passages that describe large geographical areas and thousands of years of geological history. But more often Zahler chooses to describe the vast in terms of the particular as in this paragraph:

"The other property owner with permission to be at the lake was Harry Truman, the 83-year-old lodge owner who became a folk hero by virtue of his stubborn refusal to leave his home of 54 years. The mud and rock and gas flowed over the shore and into Spirit Lake, leaving no sign of Harry Truman, his lodge, his 16 cats or his player piano."

Find other such examples and discuss the effectiveness of this approach.

A conversation with
Richard Zahler

CLARK: It would be fair to describe this as the story of a lifetime for a reporter. An incredible event, and a wonderful opportunity for a writer. Why don't you take me through the whole process of how this story was developed.

ZAHLER: The first small eruptions had started in March, and I had been down in that area and had done things as a first hand reporter and as a rewrite man. The big one happened on Sunday morning, May 18. I was scheduled to begin two weeks of vacation. But I was called in and spent the whole day organizing our coverage. I had set up our disaster coverage plan a few weeks earlier: long detailed lists of who goes where, phone numbers, how you get a rental car, all the things you worry about. Then when this happened, at 8:30 on a Sunday morning, suddenly it was all worthless because everything was closed, people were home in bed. So I spent the first four hours getting reporters in the field, and reserving airplanes, and running down rental cars hundreds of miles away. I spent the rest of the day — it turned out to be an 18 hour day — rewriting. Stuff was coming in on the wires. We had five reporter-photographer teams in the field. I spent a lot of time organizing the coverage and doing the first day writing.

How did you decide to retell the whole story a week later?

Late Wednesday evening, the editors decided that we would put out a special section on the eruption and its effects for the following Sunday.

We knew this would be the type of story never attempted by the *Seattle Times* before. When you have a big event and you want to cover it in a big way, there's a tendency to do a story, put together about four pages with a bunch of pictures and three or four sidebars. And you miss the whole thrust of the thing. This was an epic event and I somehow wanted to convey that in words. I suggested it early in the week and on Wednesday the production decision was made. Given the production demands I would have to come in on Thursday morning and work 24 hours straight.

When you came in on Thursday how did you begin?

I had this huge stack of wire stories, pages torn out of our paper, pages torn out of other papers, that accumulated in an immense mound under my desk. I put a sign on it that the janitors should leave it alone. On Thursday morning I started going through it, throwing most of it away as too general for my needs. It didn't have the specific, vivid kind of information I was looking for. Ultimately, I gleaned out of it a small stack I wanted to use for reference.

You were looking for new people, new stories, fresh information?

I had this sense of commitment. I didn't want to just retread some stuff for the readers that they had already read about all week. The eruption in general they knew about. I wanted to find fresh stories to tell them about people caught in the middle of this and how they responded and give a very personal look at the course of that one day. Then there was the question of practicality. What could be done was a key question, given the time frame and the amount of work to be done. The key thing was to be able to write a hell of a story.

Let's talk about reporting. OK, so you've got about four hours under your belt, 20 to go.

I sat down and made a list of what hadn't been covered right, what we didn't have good details on. I started coming up with a series of highly specific assignments. The first was for a reporter to get to the weather bureau and find out exactly what the weather was at 8:30 on Sunday morning at about 15 different towns that might come into my narrative. What the temperature was, what the visibility was, what the forecast and the winds were. I wasn't quite sure how I was going to use this, but I didn't want to reach the point in the narrative where I'd have to say: Gee, I wonder what the weather was. I wound up not using it in any specific way but it gave me a general perception as to how I would write the lead. A perfectly beautiful day up in this part of the country. Just a lovely, lovely day. Then all hell broke loose.

The story works out better on a lovely day, doesn't it?

Yeah, if it had been thundery and miserable, who would have cared? (Laughs.) The romanticists called it the irony of nature or something like that.

The pathetic fallacy.

There you go. I've looked for that term. That's it. From there I tried to isolate people I knew we could get to on the telephone. We worked it out directly. One of the early sections of the narrative would recount the experiences of a small town minister. This thing was just on top of him on Sunday morning when everyone is supposed to be getting ready for church. It's a beautiful Sunday morning. Peace and order should prevail in the world. I knew that this thing would be coming in there about 9:30 or 10 o'clock and dis-

rupt a whole Sunday morning. So I asked a reporter to find a small town minister in that place
and get him to talk about that morning.

**So you came up with the idea that the min-
ister would be a good person for the story
even before you found that particular guy?**

It was an isolating process. First I wanted to get
someone in this town, then look at the time
frame. Well, let's talk to a minister. Some of
these ideas didn't work out. But some did. At
some point I said: Find a person who wound up
with a whole bunch of refugees in his house in
this stranded, ash-ridden place in eastern Washington and get a reporter on the phone and start
making the calls till he comes up with that person. I talked to the mayor of Spokane who had to
deal with this. I ran him through his whole day,
what he did in the morning, what he was wearing, what he ate for breakfast. We were working
on the phone at this point. I had asked reporters
who had been out in the field to go through their
notebooks and find me little details that might
not have gotten into their stories. But mostly it
was fresh reporting: Getting on the phone, finding the guy you wanted, spending an hour talking about that day.

**Well, those reporters did a heck of a job.
They really asked the type of question that
elicited useful chunks of narrative.**

That was partly skilled reporting and partly
some coaching on my part. I wanted to have the
type of information I would be able to use if I were
writing a piece of fiction. Descriptions of what
these guys looked like, what size shoe did they
wear, what were they doing at this very moment,
when did they go from here to there and what
were they thinking about, take them in great detail through the day.

What were your reporters doing? Typing out their notes and handing them in?

This all came down to an immense pile of type-written notes, just pages and pages of it.

You've got stuff coming in from five reporters, you've got notes you've collected from other reporters during the week, plus the small pile of material culled from the junk under your desk.

That's my working material. And it was about six o'clock Thursday night. About 12 hours to go. I just had to sit down, pull it all together, and write the hell out of it.

Let's talk about the lead or introduction. Is that what magazine writers call a billboard?

Yes, in effect. There's nothing provocative or experimental about the form of the lead. First I wanted to describe nature gone amuck on a day that you would have expected anything but. So I had the pathetic fallacy, now that you've given me the right word for it, clearly in my mind. And using that billboard technique, I tried to salt in some of those people I'm going to refer to later. You can't appreciate the eruption unless you've seen this damn thing. The effects in terms of geography are just incredible. The whole damn state was just covered with this stuff coming out of the sky. I wanted to give a sense of people. Just bang, all of a sudden, here it was. I wanted to give a feeling of broad geography and that this was a story that began millions of years ago.

It sounds sort of Micheneresque.

I guess it is, isn't it? But I had that in mind, too, I think. Try to deal with these fundamental realities and build on them.

What is the function of the billboard? What sort of things was this first page and a half designed to do?

With that technique you're hinting that there's some dramatic stuff to come and you're setting that up. You get people doing something in the opening, and then later you have their circumstances drastically and dramatically changed. Everybody knows the eruption has taken place. So there are no surprises. But you can still skillfully work for that sense of drama, even though everybody knows what it's all about.

Your lead is both a menu and a promise to the reader.

I like the promise part of it better than the menu part. You're promising that there is a dramatic story here. Stick around, it's going to be fun.

So what you're doing is focusing the material in this lead. You're setting up, or foreshadowing, or promising things which will develop later in the narrative.

One of the narrative techniques that goes on here, and it starts in the opening: It builds to periodic climaxes. Each section builds up to a dramatic point and drops back and we start building to a new climax. And the new climax is the eruption and its effects. You drop off again and start telling somebody else's story and you bring him to the point of the eruption.

Why did you decide on that particular structure? Contrast that to the way the *Philadelphia Inquirer* handled Three Mile Island, telling the whole thing in chronological order.

Each section is in chronological order, but the narrative periodically steps back and starts over again. I'm telling a series of individual stories.

The other possible structure was to keep all of these players moving at once as everything develops. I chose not to do that because it would have been a lot more difficult under the time pressure.

Are you writing one full draft all the way through?

Essentially. The glory of working on electronic terminals is you can refine things as you go along, and there's a couple of hundred inches of copy here.

Did you work from an outline?

I always use an outline on longer, complex pieces. It's not a formal outline, but I have a clear view of the order I want things, and where I want to be when I end up.

Give me an idea of how that would work with this material. Did you divide it into categories and subcategories?

I riffled through a stack of notes like a deck of cards. It was all in one big pile, but I had it so I could peel through it as I needed after I made an outline. I did the outline first. I knew what material was there. I knew whose stories I had. The outline is no more than: Intro (yet to be written), Geology becomes the second section, next something like Eruption History, then it gets into individual stories of what happened on the day of the eruption. I decided to alternate the stories between the scene around the volcano where there was greatest devastation, to step away and look at what was happening as this immense ash cloud was descending on the state. Day turning gradually to night. If you had been in a satellite observatory it would have been spectacular to watch this black blot across the Northwest.

As I hear you describe it, this thing is so remarkable, that I would think that cinematic scenes would flash through your mind. I don't know, scenes from *The Ten Commandments*, the plagues of Egypt. Was that happening at all?

Absolutely (laughs). You have to do it. Disaster coverage is a staple in this business, but here we have an unprecedented disaster, no one has ever covered anything like this. We didn't have any cliches to write about this with. We've certainly developed them since. People were at a loss for words during the first hours. There was nothing in the vocabulary of our profession to deal with it. And that made for some fine writing. People turned in creative prose in trying to come to grips with this. The story doesn't need any embellishment. Whole forests flattened in a few seconds.

This story has more startling details than almost any other news story I can think of. Fish jumping out of rivers. Forests flattened. Old Harry Truman disappearing from the face of the earth. Is there a different sort of challenge when you have so much good material to work with?

There was an amazing amount of detail, things that you couldn't believe. Within the limits of time and space I was trying to choose the best of it, to somehow convey an intelligible understanding of what had happened.

There's a lot of technical information, geology and meteorology, that you had to deal with. Did you have trouble weaving that into a narrative?

That's mostly the experience of literature. I'm a strong believer in story telling as story telling. The thing has got to move and develop. It's got to have detail and real people and feeling and emotion. You've got to work hard to get what you need: what people wear, what happens to their faces when a certain emotion occurs.

Did you find yourself translating lots of technical jargon for your reader?

We've got a good science reporter here. He had already taken the technical information and produced some very readable stuff that a general audience would understand. He had a good file on that. He was more faithful to the precise scientific outlook while I was more literary with it.

What's the secret of writing so effectively on deadline?

The mistake that most people make when they are writing on deadline is that they think they can dispense with planning and organizing. I mean taking three or four minutes before you start, to think about the material you have, what you want to cover. When I'm writing on deadline, except in the most extreme cases, I take that three or four minutes to make a quick list of the high points of the story and to organize my thinking before I write.

Thomas Plate
Deadline Writing

THOMAS PLATE is associate editor and editor of the editorial pages of the *Los Angeles Herald Examiner*. He writes most of the newspaper's editorials on national and international politics. At the age of 36, Plate has already had a distinguished and varied writing career. Before coming to Los Angeles, Plate worked for *New York* magazine, *Newsday* and *Newsweek*. He has written four books: *Understanding Doomsday*, a study of the SALT talks; *Crime Pays!*, a study of the American underworld; and *Commissioner*, a study of American police behavior. He will publish a novel about the West Coast underworld under a pseudonym. He has written a fifth book with his wife, Andrea Darvi, on internal security organizations in Third World countries. He is a graduate of Amherst College and has a graduate degree in international affairs from Princeton University.

Tonight Reagan's speech, tomorrow the campaign trail

JULY 17, 1980

DETROIT — It was an extraordinary, melodramatic evening, ending in the nomination of Ronald Reagan for the presidency. And early today it was a better-than-ordinary, if anticlimactic, press conference, unveiling the national GOP ticket of Reagan and George Bush for the TV cameras. And so as this 34th National Republican Convention turns for home, with only the formalities of the acceptance speeches tonight, the GOP looks to a grueling fall campaign against President Jimmy Carter and Vice President Walter Mondale.

Even the prospect of debates arose when Reagan announced he had received a telephone call from President Carter prior to the morning press conference. "He expressed the hope that several times during the campaign we could debate, and I said I looked forward to that," said Reagan, who said he also wanted to debate independent presidential candidate John B. Anderson.

But Reagan/Bush almost didn't happen. They almost didn't become an item. For at least several hours yesterday, a seemingly endless expanse of tension, it looked like Ronald Reagan was entertaining a better idea than Bush and his name was Gerald Ford.

But it turned out to be the ticket that even Ronald Reagan couldn't get, and it was Reagan himself, in an act of both considerable grace and probably also considerable fatigue, who made the announcement. He was whisked by limousine from his heavily guarded compound on the 69th floor of the Detroit Plaza Hotel and entered the steamy, packed and emotionally confused Joe Louis Arena to the deafening roar of virtually every man and woman crammed in the place.

HERALD EXAMINER

"I know I am breaking precedent to come here tonight," said the GOP's 1980 nominee for president, ". . . but I felt it necessary to break tradition. . . . It is true a number of Republican leaders . . . felt as I am sure many of you felt . . . that a ticket should include former President Gerald Ford.

"It is also true that we have gone over this and over this and over this and he (Ford) and I have come to the conclusion . . . that he can be of more value as a former president campaigning his heart out . . . and not as a member of the ticket . . ."

With that, the 1980 Republican National Convention was practically over—and George Bush, the ex-everything, politically rose from the ashes of the politically passed-on.

And so tonight, after the usual preliminaries, the two GOP candidates who hope to replace Jimmy Carter and Walter Mondale in the White House will deliver their acceptance speeches, and the convention will be history.

But it will be history in flux, because the ink has not yet dried on this suddenly extraordinary political convention. It has not dried because what should have been, or could have been, a cut-and-dried convention turned, in the waning hours of its next-to-last day, into one of the most bizarre conventions in memory.

On some objective scale of relative historical measurement, it may even have surpassed the stunning 1960 Democratic National Convention in Los Angeles, when totally out of the blue, John F. Kennedy chose as his running mate his bitter political foe, the tall, wheeling-dealing Southerner, Lyndon Johnson.

It was a feat of political risk-taking that, in a sense, Reagan tried to duplicate last night. He reached for his Lyndon Johnson, but his reach exceeded his grasp.

Gerald Ford turned out to be no Lyndon Johnson. Apparently by setting his acceptance preconditions too steep for Reagan to meet, the

former president turned down a chance to regain
a job he once held, a job which Vice President
John Nance Garner once described as not worth
"a pitcher of warm spit," and a job which, come
January, may find as its occupant George Bush,
who last night lavished praise on Reagan in the
best-received speech so far at the convention.

Had the selection of Bush not been preceded
by revelations about the tortuous *pas de deux*
with former President Ford, Reagan and his inner circle of advisers huddled here in Detroit
might have won the plaudits of most seasoned political observers, including the media pundits
and the professional consultants.

For the selection of Bush, standing on its
own merits, was thought here in many political
circles to add great strength to the ticket, to
"broaden the base," in the cliched language of
the political pundits, and to take the sting out of
the arrogant rebuff to women voters on both the
Equal Rights Amendment and abortion issue.

But the selection of Bush occurred not in an orderly, intellectual vacuum, but in a vortex of political deal-making and deal-breaking that has left all involved here practically gasping for air. To be sure, after the dust has settled, the public and the press will settle themselves down to examining the candidates and the issues. But there will be a period of time, inevitably, when the most discussed aspect of the Reagan-Bush ticket will be the Reagan-Ford ticket that almost was.

And the public discussion will center inevitably on how Ronald Reagan—conservative, careful, well-staffed Ronald Reagan—could have gone down to the wire at this convention only to trip at the finish line.

For it is clear that last night was Ronald Reagan's Schweiker all over again. The liberal Richard Schweiker of Pennsylvania was picked by Reagan in advance of the Kansas City convention four years ago to be his running mate in a move that infuriated many conservatives and left the nation wondering whether Reagan hadn't reached so far across the political spectrum as to raise doubts about his plausibility.

And last night he did it again—he appeared to have overreached himself. But this time the charge was not that he made his move too early. The charge was that he may have made his move too late.

So late in the game, in fact, that after George Bush gave his speech and left the convention hall, he returned to his suite of hotel rooms at the nearby Pontchartrain Hotel utterly convinced that the chalice had passed his lips and had been handed to Gerald Ford to enjoy.

Will the whole unforgettable incident go down as a definitive blunder that raised the disturbing questions about the Republican candidate's decision-making (and deal-making) abilities—questions that the Democrats are sure to raise at their convention in New York? Or will the incident be ultimately forgotten, a victim to

PLATE   81

the inherent wisdom that many political observers here feel was the choice of a moderate
like George Bush?

No one in Detroit last night had the answers. Everyone was still catching his breath.
It was the night when the so-called Reagan-Ford
dream turned into a nightmare.

Observations and questions

1) In "Politics and The English Language," George
Orwell suggests that writers should avoid figures
of speech they are used to seeing in print. Of the
following phrases used by Plate, which seem fresh
and which seem stale? Examine your own writing
and make the same judgments:

> He was whisked by limousine
> deafening roar
> George Bush, the ex-everything
> rose from the ashes
> because the ink has not yet dried
> out of the blue
> the tortuous *pas de deux* with former Presi-
>   dent Ford
> after the dust has settled
> gone down to the wire
> late in the game
> the chalice had passed his lips

Attempt to rewrite the expressions that you
think are cliches. Show your revision and the
original to a friend. Which does he like better
and why?

2) There was a companion story to this one covering the unsuccessful attempt to get Gerald Ford
on the Republican ticket. With that in mind, do
you think that Plate gives the Ford element
enough emphasis? Recall how television handled
the Ford story. Contrast television's approach to
Plate's.

Carter upstaged twice—
by Mondale and Kennedy

AUGUST 15, 1980

NEW YORK — It was not a speech that will live in history. But the night might. It was the night that the President of the United States, accepting the nomination of his party for re-election, was upstaged.

And last night—a night that should have been all his to enjoy—he was upstaged twice in succession, possibly a new record of some kind for modern-day presidents.

First he was outdone by his own vice president. The simple fact was that Walter Mondale gave a much better speech than his running mate. Like an up-and-coming executive beating his boss at a game of tennis, Vice President Mondale served an ace right down the middle of the emotion of this convention with a rollicking, energetic, almost Ted Kennedy-like demonstration of political oratory.

But the second undoing was far more serious than the first. Everyone wondered how the president of the United States would manage to follow Sen. Kennedy's magnificent Tuesday night performance.

Well, last night the nation got its answer. President Carter couldn't follow Sen. Kennedy's Tuesday night act, but Sen. Kennedy could.

In one of the most brutal and quietly vicious snubs in recent political memory, the almost-nominee arrived quite late on the dais, looked for all the world as if he were in the most uncomfortable pain, spent the minimum amount of time decently possible on the podium, managed at best a puerile smile and limp handshake for the president, avoided the traditional arms-raised-in-victory platform pose of all-in-the-Democratic-family-reunited, and slipped off the platform into

PLATE   83

the crowd of delegates as if a man wishing to a-
void contagion.

It was a real stunner, a dark and foreboding
act of political revenge by a man who did what he
was asked to do by a president whom he must really in his heart despise. Maybe in a few weeks,
or months, the bitterness will evaporate in the
steamy struggle against a man they both hate in
common: Ronald Reagan. Maybe.

But surely for President Carter, the bitterness lingered long into the night, as he made his
way back to his suite at the Sheraton Centre hotel some 10 blocks away, possibly to lick his
wounds and possibly to reflect on the fact that he
delivered one of the most lackluster acceptance
speeches that many political observers here
could remember for some time.

For if Kennedy's Tuesday night speech
lasted 33 minutes but seemed to sweep by in a
flash of galvanized emotion, and if Vice President Mondale's short speech last night seemed to
ride past the delegates in a quick series of orator-
ical waves, Jimmy Carter's speech last night
seemed to last for about 53 hours.

If it was not the most ineffective speech in
some time, it seemed a mark of singular unorig-
inality. The attacks on Reagan were hard, but
uninspired, except for a line or two (neither of
which will live in history). The defense of his administration seemed too defensive. And the appeal to understanding seemed genuflective and
possibly even insincere, as if the president were
going through the motions rather than riding on
to victory.

Even the necessary encomiums to his former Democratic rival seemed about as sincere as
the president's smile when he greeted Sen. Kennedy on the podium.

"Ted, you're a tough competitor and a superb
campaigner," Carter said in his speech last night.
"I can attest to that. . . .

"I reach out tonight to you and those who
supported you in your valiant and passionate

campaign. Ted, your party needs—and I need—your idealism and dedication working for us."

Carter did not evoke Camelot, he did not bring tears to the eyes of the delegates, he did not sweep this convention off its feet.

Instead, the president almost tripped at the starting gate, identifying the 1968 Democratic nominee for president as "Hubert Horatio Hornblower" before quickly correcting himself to "Humphrey."

Carter did not, however, have trouble remembering the precise name of his 1980 Republican opponent—or painting for his convention audience a vivid and sometimes even frightening picture of Ronald Reagan.

"I see risk," he said, in reference not to the fall campaign but to a putative Reagan presidency, "the risk of international confrontation: the risk of an uncontrollable, unaffordable and unwinnable nuclear arms race."

Was he suggesting that his Republican opponent was a warmonger?

"No one, Democrat or Republican, consciously seeks such a future. I do not claim that my opponent does. But I do question the disturbing commitments and policies already made by him and by those with him who have already captured control of the Republican Party.

"The consequences of those commitments and politics would drive us down the wrong road. It is up to all of us to make sure America rejects this alarming, even perilous, destiny."

The words he chose to describe Reagan were choice indeed. Reaganites, he said, live "in their fantasy world," "have simple solutions—simple and wrong," sound "too good to be true" and propose "a make-believe world of good guys and bad guys where some politicians shoot first and ask questions later."

The words were not those of James Earl Carter the President of the United States but those of Jimmy Carter the gutty, street-fighting political campaigner.

PLATE   85

He ridiculed what he described as Reagan's "tough-sounding talk." Said the president, in a line that got one of the better responses from the delegates on the floor, "he is not sure if he wants to feed them (the Russians), play with them or fight with them"—an obvious reference to the Republican nominee's opposition to the Soviet grain embargo, draft registration and the Moscow Olympics boycott.

He attacked the Republican National Convention's planks on the Equal Rights Amendment (applause here), the Kemp-Roth tax cut, energy policy, foreign policy, farm policy, labor policy and, more than once, arms control policies. Invoking the names of Truman and even Eisenhower, he said that the Republicans' "radical and irresponsible course would threaten our security—and could put the whole world in peril. You and I must never let this come to pass."

Yes, the president was suggesting that his opponent might be some kind of warmonger.

"It is a choice between two futures. The year 2000 is less than 20 years away—just four presidential elections after this one. Children born this year will come of age in the 21st century"—if, the president seemed to be saying, a Reagan-triggered nuclear apocalypse does not beat the 21st century to the punch.

But even while he was painting his opponent as a latter-day Barry Goldwater, the president was not painting himself as a Southern version of a Northern liberal. There was the traditional commitment to "economic security"—"the justice of good jobs, decent health care and quality of education," "human rights for all men—and for all women" and "a peace guaranteed both by American military strength and by American moral strength."

But there was, of course, no mention of the $12 billion jobs program, or wage-and-price controls, or any of the other minority planks on which he and Edward Kennedy had fought for position these past few days in New York.

Instead, while attacking Ronald Reagan as Jimmy the campaigner, he also presented himself as James Earl Carter the president.

"I have learned that only the most complex and difficult tasks end up in the Oval Office," he said. "No easy answers are found there—because no easy questions come there."

"I am a wiser man tonight than I was four years ago ... A president cannot yield to the shortsighted demands of special interests, no matter how rich and powerful they are. This is why the president cannot bend to the passions of the moment, no matter how popular they are."

The Nov. 4 election offers, he insisted, "a stark choice between two men, two parties, two sharply different pictures of America and the world ... We are going to whip the Republicans in November."

And that, in the words of the White House aides who labored over this acceptance speech since May, was Jimmy Carter's "best speech."

PLATE   87

It may have been, but it was not the speech that Edward Kennedy gave on Tuesday night. It was a Jimmy Carter speech—combative, self-justifying, at times almost pious—and was delivered not with the rolling cadences of the polished orator or even the polished Baptist minister, but in jabs and punches, with feints to the right and then to the left.

And there may be a lesson in this: For if Ronald Reagan has staked out his turf in a way that is clearly visible to friend and foe alike, President Carter's performance last night was more difficult to label. Was it conservative? Was it liberal? Was it hawkish? Dovish?

His speech seemed to suggest, surely by design, that he is in fact all of these, because he is in fact the president of the United States and the only president we have.

And Ronald Reagan is not the president, should not be the president, may even be a closet warmonger, may be a radical reactionary and may be beaten, if the president's party unites around his candidacy.

But the party was very late in uniting. It wasn't until late Wednesday night that the president received word of Sen. Kennedy's support. And it wasn't until early yesterday that Carter learned of the senator's decision to share the podium. And when the time came for the senator to join the nominee on the podium, Sen. Kennedy was late again, almost embarrassingly late. A symbolic act? Or just caught in traffic? Or both? Somehow, it seemed the story of this surprisingly difficult and testy Democratic convention.

Observations and questions

1) Howell Raines of the *New York Times* talks of the need to write about politicians as human characters rather than authority figures. In what ways does Plate deal with Carter and Kennedy as human characters? What are their strengths and weaknesses in this scene? Is there a "subtext" which reveals important character flaws?

2) Raines also says that political writers should give "new information" to the reader. Can you identify in Plate's story facts that you would not get from standard television or newspaper coverage? In what ways is Plate interpreting television for the reader?

3) Try this experiment: Attend an event (a session of the legislature or an athletic event or a convention) and write a story about it. Then watch a similar event on television and write another story. Consider and discuss the different perspectives that come from seeing it on television and attending it in person.

4) John McPhee compares a lead to a flashlight that shines down into the story, illuminating what is to come. Examine Plate's lead. Does it adequately prepare us for what is to follow?

5) This might be described as a piece of news analysis. Go through the story carefully with a pencil and identify those places where Plate goes beyond observation to judgment. Be sure to examine the language Plate uses to describe the Carter-Kennedy confrontation on the podium:
   ". . .as if he were in the most uncomfortable pain."

PLATE   89

". . .managed . . . a puerile smile and limp
hand shake."

". . .as if a man wishing to avoid contagion."

6) Plate uses some words seldom seen in newspaper writing: *puerile, genuflective, galvanized, en-
comium, putative* and *apocalypse*. Do you have to
look up these words, or do you understand them
from context? Some editors might criticize these
words as too "fancy" for a newspaper story. What
do you think? Look through your own recent stories. Can you find places in which you could have
replaced words that you used with more appropriate ones? Orwell says never use a long
word where a short one will do. Can you substi-
tute shorter, better words for long ones you have
used?

7) There's a temptation to think of political strug-
gles in terms of other types of fights, races or con-
tests. Examine these phrases and discuss whether they help us understand political realities.

". . .like an up and coming executive beating
his boss at a game of tennis."

". . .the president almost tripped at the
starting gate."

". . .Jimmy Carter, the gutty, street fighting
political campaigner."

". . .Ronald Reagan has staked out his turf."

Reagan leads GOP romp, winning big everywhere

NOVEMBER 5, 1980

It was a night in which American history seemed to turn on its heels toward the Republicans.

In an absolutely stunning and wholly unexpected landslide that had devastating reverberations on races all over the country, including some here in Los Angeles, the voters of the United States said, not in a tentative whisper but in a virtual shout, that it was time for a drastic change. By the smashing margin of 463 electoral votes to 75, they ordered that on Jan. 20 the mantle of the office of the presidency of the United States will be turned over to former California Gov. Ronald Reagan, an avowed enemy of traditional liberal Democratic policies, a Westerner and, at 69, the oldest man ever to become president.

For president James Earl Carter, the night was a nightmare. The popular vote was about 51 percent for Reagan, 42 percent for Carter and 6% for Rep. John Anderson, but the election wasn't even as close, really, as that. The president was expected to lose the West, which he did, but he wasn't expected to lose the East, which he did. The Midwest had been thought to be up for grabs, but no one expected that the president would lose everything in the South except his native Georgia. What it all added up to, by night's end, was that Jimmy Carter had lost almost everywhere, and had lost so big that overnight he had become the first elected incumbent president in almost five decades to suffer defeat at the polls—when in 1932 FDR crushed Herbert Hoover and ushered in the New Deal. Even Adlai Stevenson, in his 1952 thumping by Ike, got more electoral votes.

A similar new epoch may have been ushered

PLATE   91

in last night. At last count, eight seats in the U.S.
Senate formerly held by Democrats fell into the
hands of Republicans last night. If one more seat
were to fall to the Republicans in a late count or
recount, it would amount to a shift that gives
control of the Senate to the Republican Party—
for the first time since Dwight David Eisenhower
was in the White House. Moving to Republican
hands, as a consequence, would be the chairman-
ships of such powerful Senate committees as agriculture, appropriations, banking, finance, energy, foreign relations and the judiciary.

And in the U.S. House of Representatives,
the Democrats, though retaining majority control, took a staggering loss of some 34 seats to the
Republicans. While the Democrats still remain
in control of the lower house, the narrowing of
the margin sets up a possibly decisive show-
down in the House elections of 1982.

Stars fell from the political sky last night in
shocking clusters. Defeated were such luminar-
ies as South Dakota's George McGovern, Iowa's
John Culver, Idaho's Frank Church, Washington's Warren Magnuson, New York's Jacob Ja-
vits, and Indiana's Birch Bayh—an incredible
roster of ousted liberals. On the House side, the
fallen stars included Indiana's John Brademas,
the House whip; Al Ullman, the Oregon Democrat who is chairman of the House Ways and
Means Committee; and Harold T. Jackson, the
Californian who is chairman of the House Public
Works Committee.

Other losers that night were four of the five
congressmen indicted in the widely publicized
Abscam investigation conducted by the FBI; only
indicted Rep. Raymond Lederer (D-Pa.) survived.

And still other losers included the major
polling organizations. None of them, for reasons
still unexplained, was able to call the huge Republican sweep, most saying right down to the
wire yesterday the election was too close to call.

And here in California, there were survivors
and there were overnight stars. Among the nota-

ble survivors were Sen. Alan Cranston, who bucked the nationwide anti-liberal trend by defeating conservative Republican Paul Gann; and conservative Republican Rep. Robert Dornan, winner over second-time challenger Carey Peck, a Democrat. Among the biggest new stars locally were conservative Republican David Dreier, successfully unseating 35th District incumbent Rep. Jim Lloyd; conservative Republican Ed Davis, the former LAPD chief who won election to the state Senate; Republican-backed Deane Dana, the winner over Yvonne Burke for the Fourth supervisorial seat; and Michael D. Antonovich, the conservative Republican who edged out longtime supervisor Baxter Ward for the Fifth supervisorial seat.

THE CARTER COLLAPSE

The president's loss last night was so total that it will stagger the imagination of analysts for weeks to come. The breakdown occurred in

PLATE   93

every section of the country, among most socio-economic groups and among most age groups. According to an ABC News exit poll conducted yesterday, Reagan won the young people, the middle-aged and the over-50. He won the protestants (by a large margin), the Catholics (narrowly) and barely lost the Jewish vote. According to the exit poll, he cut heavily into the union vote, heavily into the unemployed vote, and even well into the self-employed vote. Reagan also scored heavily among voters with a college education or more.

Among male voters, according to ABC, Reagan murdered Carter, but among female voters, expected to go heavily for Carter, Reagan more than held his own. Only black voters went for Carter, roughly 4-1.

But perhaps most telling of all, voters seemed to vote against Carter as much as they voted for Reagan. It was an anti-Carter vote that had coattails for many Republicans, to be sure, but it did come across as a huge anti-Carter referendum. In the ABC exit poll, those who voted against the president said they did so because of his inadequacies in the areas of (a) inflation, (b) foreign affairs, and (c) government spending. These were the major issues taken up by Gov. Reagan, and it now seems in hindsight that the governor picked them very well indeed.

The governor also stayed away from the hostage issue the last week, but it seems that for all the speculation about how the president may have been trying to maneuver this crisis to his political benefit, in fact the latest maneuvering with Khomeini and the Islamic revolutionary government probably cut against the president. Said Robert Strauss, the chairman of the re-election campaign committee: "The events of the last four days, the Iranian hostages, they came down on us. It brought back all the frustrations of the last year."

In the end, the underlying issue may have been Carter's basic competence. And even last night, the issue was raised anew. The occasion was his concession speech. The president delivered it on national television out of Washington, where the polls had closed. But the polls hadn't closed out West, and as the president formally conceded, Democrats up and down the West coast, from Washington's Warren Magnuson to L.A.'s Yvonne Burke, were loudly complaining that the president's premature concession may have cost the Democratic Party out here important, desperately needed votes.

THE REAGAN TRIUMPH

It was nothing short of sensational. It began in the South, rolled north up to the north Midwest, turned east as the polls closed in Connecticut, New Jersey and Pennsylvania, and roared west toward Reagan country in a devastating floodtide for Reaganism.

In retrospect, the Republican nominee turned a squeaker into a laugher. How he did it will surely be the subject of admiring analyses for weeks to come. Some will say the turn came a week ago yesterday in Cleveland, when Ronald Reagan stood next to Jimmy Carter and seemed a taller figure in more ways than one. Others will point to the sad, enervating hostage crisis and attribute Reagan's win to Khomeini's heartless outmaneuvering of Carter. Still others will attribute the landslide to voting against the idea that the Iranians may have tried in their own clumsy way to tilt the election toward Carter. And, to be sure, many will point to the troubled state of the economy.

But perhaps, in the mind of many voters, the rise of the Republicans began four years ago, when a relatively unknown one-term ex-governor from Georgia tried to do the job of president and, to the perception of both allies abroad and citizens at home, did not seem up to the job. However fair or unfair the appraisal, the beneficiary of the perception last night was yet another former governor untested in federal service: Ronald Reagan.

Observations and questions

1) Writing an election night story on deadline is a challenging task for any writer, especially on the night of a presidential election. Examine this piece closely. How does Plate balance facts with analysis?

2) Placement is a key element of emphasis for a journalist. Where does Plate place information on national, state and local politics in this story? Do you agree with his judgments?

3) Reread the sections called "The Carter Collapse" and "The Reagan Triumph." In light of what you now know, does Plate's analysis hold up?

4) Books on style encourage the writer to avoid unnecessary adjectives and adverbs. The key word is *unnecessary*—which is a necessary adjective. Read Plate's second paragraph. Look at the words *absolutely, wholly, tentative, virtual, drastic, smashing, avowed*. Which seem necessary, which excessive? Read William Zinsser's book *On Writing Well* (New York: Harper & Row, 1976). Study what he has to say about removing clutter and apply some of his techniques to your work.

5) After reading these pieces do you have any sense of Plate's feelings about Carter and Reagan? Do they seem accurate, fair, balanced? If you think so, discuss the approaches to the writing that persuade you.

A conversation with
Tom Plate

CLARK: "The night President Carter was upstaged" was a particularly effective piece of political analysis. Tell me how you did that one.

PLATE: It came toward the end of convention week when I was getting tired. I wanted to have my story of that day written in advance to give LA a breather technically. So I wrote this OK story, sent it to LA and said: 'I'll retop it if I have to.' Then I saw Ted Kennedy on the podium and that amazing behavior and I called Mary Anne Dolan, our managing editor. I said: Mary Anne, did you see what I saw. Maybe I ought to retop the story. She said, I think you ought to rewrite it completely. She was right. I wrote it, it appeared in the paper the next day, and she called to say, "I want you to know that was one of the most marvelous pieces of political writing I've ever seen." I'm looking at stories in the *New York Times* and in other papers, and they missed it. They missed the emotion of it. That is what I'm trying to get at in all these convention stories. To get at the essential emotion. Conventions are not only products of calculation. They are products of intense emotion. That piece was the essence of deadline writing, which is to say that it could not be written at three in the afternoon. It could only be written at 10 o'clock at night.

Because you were in the heat? Because you were right on top of it?

You have to be on top of it emotionally and intellectually. The key is psychological preparation, which to me involves two things: knowing everything that you can know and reading everything

PLATE   97

that you can read, everything I can get my hands on. The second is a kind of psyching yourself up so you can get into the flow and the emotion of the event so you can convey it to your reader. In fact, the *Herald Examiner* is not competing with the *LA Times*. It's competing with television. Television brings you something with tremendous vividness. Our advantage is that we can bring it to you with perspective and detail. But it must also have an equivalent vividness. If it doesn't, people will turn the station.

Your description of the snub of Carter by Kennedy is exceptional. Where were you when it happened?

In addition to writing these pieces, I was the bureau chief of the six people we had there. We had two floor reporters. So I was watching it on television which, in fact, is the best perspective to see any of this stuff. I said to my reporters: Could you see it (the snub) there? They said absolutely. I could see it on television. Some papers are afraid to convey the emotion of an event. So they only convey the "factual content." But emotion is a fact.

So you were trying to deal with these politicians as human characters rather than as authority figures?

There was no question in my mind that Senator Kennedy with that incredible ego, that Camelot background, incredible fortune, who felt that the presidency belonged to him, walked up on that podium and said, "I have lost to this little squirt from Georgia." And could not accept it. That's what I was writing about.

You were also forthright about reporting Carter's flub of Hubert Humphrey's name. I saw some political reporters who seemed to overlook that.

Because of the tremendous technological revolution brought on by television, one of the things that newspapers must do is explain what you have seen on television. Like going behind the screen. In other words, if the president makes an incredible flub like that — or there is a seeming expression of arrogance on the face of Ted Kennedy, and he just barely shakes the president's hand, and he stays there for a record 2.3 seconds, and stalks off in a huff like somebody stole his beachball — and you don't explain it, then the story has diminished reality in the eyes of the reader.

Would you call these pieces exercises in "explanatory journalism"?

That sounds too didactic. We came up with a new term. We called them "sweep" pieces. I like the term "sweep" because it gives you a sense of completeness and a kind of emotion. You're going to get the sweep like the opening of *Gone with the Wind* or a Tolstoy novel. You're going to get the color, the political analysis, the historical background, a feel for the leading protagonist of that event.

Is there a conspiracy of silence among political reporters to keep certain things out of the newspaper?

Reporters tend to be fairly patriotic, but that's a plus. There are several reasons why some information doesn't get in the paper. I was just in London for two months. There was a reporter there who has covered Parliament for 17 years. He knows everything that goes on in Parliament. And he knows things that ought to be in the story or things the editors ought to know to help shape coverage. He sometimes doesn't bring it to the surface, in part because he's so familiar with the material, it doesn't seem like news to him. A lot of political stuff is tremendously gossipy and de-

PLATE   99

velops a fictional life of its own. When you examine it, it can't be put in a newspaper because it's often quite exaggerated.

How do you make sense of the complexities of a convention or an election night? How do you get control over it? As the evening progresses do you start developing hypothetical versions of the story?

In my mind I do. It's almost like a computer. Say to the computer, there are 565 permutations here. Run through them all. I run through as many as I can, sifting and sorting through leads, different approaches. But there must be no confusion in my mind when I sit down at the typewriter. You must be both complete and selective, so that your story will be an all-embracing thing. But it also has a tunnel vision, so you start at the beginning of the tunnel, go through it, and in fact you do get to the light at the end of the tunnel.

I've heard somebody say that brevity comes from selection, not compression.

The selection comes from doing an enormous amount of work for the reader. The reader can look at the story and say, OK, I can trust this guy because he's really done a lot of work on the story and that's why I'm paying 25¢ for the paper.

I've also heard someone compare a news story to an iceberg. The 10 percent above the water is what the reader sees. The 90 percent below is the research and the reporter's knowledge that supports the story.

But the reader must understand what's underneath the water. He must believe that the reporter is telling him what he needs to know.

Let's talk about the question of fairness in political reporting. Did anyone assume that

because you're from Los Angeles that you were partial to Reagan?

In the sense that he's the hometown boy, yes. We might give more space to the story about Reagan. It's the ultimate home-town-boy-makes-good story. You always root for the person who lives on your block. You root for the home team rather than the visiting team. You need to understand the context in which you're writing. A New York context is different than a Los Angeles context, different than a Washington context. It's a mistake to believe that's not the case. It's also a mistake to believe you can con the reader. Suppose Reagan had given a terrible acceptance speech, and you tell them that he gave a great speech. They saw the speech. If you assume your readers are stupid, you're out of business.

Couldn't a reporter who was more sympathetic to Carter have handled the upstaging story to show Carter in a more favorable light?

If you go in with any preconceived political perspective, you can say the color isn't red, the color is black. But unless you're close to the reality of the situation, you're going to lose your credibility. What Carter should have done was not accept that sort of thing from Kennedy. Just tell him: You're gonna shake my hand or I'm gonna walk off the stage. He is the President of the United States, and I don't care how much you hate him, he's still the president. He deserves respect and he was not shown that. And it was in the minds of the reader, "If this man can be kicked around by Ted Kennedy, he can also be kicked by Ayatollah Khomeini." That was the perception of the American public in the vote for the presidency. Reagan showed a certain sense of command. Carter had consistently shown a certain lack of command. While we didn't endorse Reagan, we were more favorable to his candidacy

PLATE 101

than to Carter's. Everything appears in that context.

I used to live in Montgomery, Alabama, when George Wallace was governor. I was impressed with the way reporters there — who had strong feelings about Wallace — could still write about him with fairness and balance.

In my recent Fleet Street (London newspaper area) experience, I am almost convinced, but not quite, that American political reporting is almost too balanced. If a reader knows that a political reporter is predisposed to be in favor of the Tories and against Labour, in a certain sense the reports in Tory papers on what happened at a Labour Party conference are going to be more valuable, precisely because they're going to be looking for the embarrassing and negative facts. By being more personal and hiding less behind the veil of objectivity, even if your story has a slant, the reader knows how to deal with it. But you cannot go too far with that. American readers are accustomed to a tradition of political objectivity where opinion and analysis are kept to the editorial page. That is a tradition you cannot fight. I'm just saying that you must not assume that tradition demands blandness.

How does a reporter deal with his or her feelings? Do you examine your feelings about a candidate before you write?

I always do that. It's a multi-layered process. Suppose a candidate makes a buffoon of himself. My emotional reaction is contempt. But how valid is that reaction? Was I predisposed to feel contempt for him? Was he in a trying situation and did the best he could? Then I ask: How many other people are likely to share that emotion? And why? You must get at the emotional component of political events because a lot of people vote from their hearts. The other thing he must do is to make the event interesting. Because if it is not interesting, then ultimately the democratic process is not interesting. If I am to be accused of propagandizing for the democratic process, I plead guilty. It's an important process of journalism to show why that form of government is valid and why it is interesting.

I hear some reporters and editors complain about local coverage of government and politics. How do you make a story interesting and relevant without hyping it? Some newspapers seem to run an endless number of boring stories about an endless number of boring governmental meetings and hearings.

If a Martian came down to earth and read just American newspapers, he would be convinced that 75 percent of American life is government. But with the exception of Washington, people live their lives with very little thought about government. They realize there is little they can do, except at elections. So their assessment is very intelligent. But they get newspapers that cover all these incredible hearings. 1) Newspapers need to take more of a news magazine approach to government. You need a Monday morning column that wraps up all that has happened in state government. A Periscope, a collection of items, done by a savvy political reporter. You don't need 30-inch stories on those things. 2) Ultimately, we need less local government stories but they need to be better. So instead of putting young reporters on them, you need to put your best writers on the stories. 3) We must constantly humanize these political stories. Who's going to be helped by this budget? Who's going to be hurt by this budget? Who's behind this budget, who's against this budget?

How do you write on deadline? Do you work from an outline?

PLATE 103

I never write an outline down on paper. All effort
to put words down must go into the story. Writing is the most difficult aspect of journalism.
That is the genius and the talent. Editors need to
marshall the genius of the writer. We are not
writing a term paper here. We are not writing a
600-page non-fiction book, which I've done. We
are writing 40-45 inches. The effort to write must
be saved for the piece. The outline must be done
in the head. You don't know exactly how things
are going to flow. The logic must come out of the
writing. It cannot be imposed in some sort of
Aristotelian sense.

**Do you write quickly? Take notes? Spend a
lot of time on your lead? How does that
work?**

You must be thinking about the piece from the
moment you get up. You will be rejecting 95 percent of all that comes into your head. But that
process of rejection is a process of refinement and
enrichment. You can write down notes, the
quotes you want to save, the observations you
may have. But the order comes at the last minute. It will come out of the logic and emotion of
the piece. Like most writers, I find that once you
get the lead, you're off and running. But not
quite. That's almost too easy. The newspaper is a
beautiful, imperfect instrument of information.
You know that and try to minimize the imperfec-
tion. So you say, OK, this piece must move to Los
Angeles in an hour and ten minutes. If you're ex-
perienced, you know what you're capable of doing in that time. You must be within yourself. It's
like a pitcher coming in with three innings to go.
He knows how many batters he's going to face,
how many hits are likely to be against him, how
many pitches he's going to throw, which batters
are dangerous. He must command the arsenal
that he has in the most effective way and be
within himself.
    If you have a 40-inch story and you have an

hour and ten minutes to do it, you know that you have a certain number of minutes per paragraph. Of the 40 paragraphs you're going to write, 10 of them are going to be quotes. So you know that when you use a quote, that buys you time. That only takes 30 seconds, so that gives you more than two minutes for another paragraph that must be written. When I'm writing on deadline like this, I know I must not write too slowly. I also must not write too fast. I don't go into the piece saying this is only a first draft, it can be terrible. I go into it saying this is going to be the last draft. Then, after I've written paragraph 40, and I have 15 minutes left, I can go back and change six. But if after I've done this first draft and have 30 minutes, and the piece is a mess, I have gained absolutely nothing.

Paul Greenberg
Commentary

PAUL GREENBERG has worked all of his newspaper career for the *Pine Bluff Commercial* in Arkansas with the exception of one year in Chicago with the *Daily News*. He was born 44 years ago in Shreveport, Louisiana, and lived there until he entered the University of Missouri. There he earned a journalism degree and a master's degree in history. He decided to pursue his graduate studies in history at Columbia University in New York City. His academic career stalled when he failed his oral examinations twice. Determined to overcome that setback, he followed the American impulse and "lit out for the territory" where he landed a job in Pine Bluff. He's spent almost 20 years in Arkansas cultivating his interest in history and trying to turn editorial writing into an art form. He won the Pulitzer Prize for editorial writing in 1969.

On the beach

AUGUST 31, 1980

SANTA ROSA ISLAND, Florida — The breakers are two to four feet high. The seawater temperature is in the 60s. High tide is at 9:16 a.m., low tide at 11:30 p.m. Westerly winds at 10 to 15 knots. The highs are in the low 90s, the lows in the 70s. Seaweed is thick. Sunrise is at 5:49 a.m., sunset at 7:55 p.m.

There is in my lap an unopened copy of *Public Opinion* by Walter Lippmann, Copyright 1922—a piece of salvage acquired on the mainland while casting about secondhand bookstores to see what sea changes might have been made in long familiar standards. One remembers the book as being earnest and sophisticated in the way of the intellectuals of the 1920s—before the 1930s knocked the stuffings out of them, and just about everybody else. The book was terribly liberal back then, with overtones of government of the few, by the better informed and for the undiscerning many.

But the book stays closed, as it has for so long. It can't compete with the waves, each and every one unique, as always. (How did He manage that one?) The waves come on unceasingly, each at its own pace, and time stops, or ceases to matter. The sound of the cool green surf rises above and apart from the far-seeing calculations of those who would shape Public Opinion, with about as much chance as shaping a wave.

I feel the need to go inside and write something, anything, even a postcard. There are those types who can't go anywhere without taking snapshots. It's the way they validate experience. They get so busy validating they may miss the experience. The pictures become more real than reality. Like the grandmother who is complimented on the grandson she's proudly wheeling around in the stroller—"Oh," she says, "you should see his picture!" The writer has his own version of the Kodak Syndrome. If the experience isn't written down, did it really happen?

Writing it down makes it intelligible, permanent, unchanging. None of which describes reality, despite the illusion of words having captured it. Reality preserved is a contradiction in terms. The words are not the experience any more than the snapshot is. What is fine language anyway but the fabrication of future cliches? These words are not what happens on the beach—there is none of the murmuring undulation of the waves in them, the serenity of the shoreline surely but almost imperceptibly changing with every wash of a wave, no ceaseless sound of the surf even when it cannot be seen in the cool of midnight, none of the sure pressure of the sunheat beating down and radiating out as though it will not, cannot stop, but has always been just like this. Like the first real heat wave of the summer felt at Fourth and Alabama in Pine Bluff, across from the old depot and among the crumbling warehouses, with the heat shimmering off the steel railroad tracks and sidewalks and concrete streets and metal parking meters and off the world everlasting itself, as though it will never let up. . . .

But reality is not in those words, either. The words are only some addictive, delusionary validation of common feelings. But to some of us they become preferable to the experience itself. Just as we hurry in off the street and away from the world to visit museums. Those who can, live. Those who can't, make pictures, or jot down endless, disconnected notes. Maybe I've been out in the sun too long.

Or maybe it's just the workings of insecurity. Like the fellow who jogs every day because he fears that if he misses just one morning, he'll never run another step. He's propelled forward not by love or challenge, or even by some fool idea

of fending off the inevitable and extending life forever, but out of simple desperation. It is anxiety made habitual, which is one description of the human condition. My wife glares at me when she sees me pick up a pencil; I'm supposed to be on vacation.

Imagine a compulsive writer who can take a vacation from writing. Like a drunk who can lay off the stuff for precisely two weeks before taking it up again on schedule. Or a politician ceasing to think of power for 14 days. Hard to imagine. Why, each one must wonder, do the others do it? What attraction is there in such an addiction? Surely the best kept secret of journalism is the insignificance of its subject.

Maybe what I need is a chapter of Writers Anonymous. But they say one must want to change for that kind of reform to work and, on a day like this, when it's too hot to think, I would rather just go on writing. Thinking is for editors in air-conditioned rooms, for neat types given to pruning kudzuvine. Right now it is too hot to link words in spurious logic, to bother with grammar and syntax and all that goes into fashioning the outward appearance of sense out of the lava flow of words on the beach. Editing is for later, like changing one's ways.

The finished product, after all the fine touches that are such bad ideas, stands like the elaborate sand castle down the way that took the better part of an afternoon to construct in all its transient glory. But those who built that had no illusions of permanence; theirs was an elaborate gesture to the passing moment, an illusion built without illusions. Theirs was an honorable and realistic undertaking compared to writing consciously for posterity.

This morning, running down a road along the beach, I came across a modest, stenciled street sign near some beach cottages. Arkansas Street, it said. Home away from home. I almost tripped over what it had replaced—a stone pillar, its concrete base uprooted and its message half covered by sand and the sea shells they use for gravel around here. "This street," it read, after I had brushed off the words, *This street is dedicated in honor of the state of ARKANSAS Admitted to the Union 1836 This plaque dedicated by Governor ORVAL E. FAUBUS 1965.* It scarcely matters now whether it was Camille or Frederick that turned over the pillar, or the more ordinary malice of time. It is still a monument of a kind, like Walter Lippmann's dusty, unread words. In the end they both pay tribute to a different reality, one without pretensions to permanence that nevertheless goes on and on, like the drifting sand and the unceasing waves.

Observations and questions

1) These pieces by Greenberg can be described as formal essays. What are the characteristics of this genre? What is the etymology of the word *essay*? How is it related to *assay*? You may want to read some examples of essays by Montaigne or E.B. White to familiarize yourself with the form. In what ways does "On the Beach" fulfill the genre?

2) Walter Lippmann's *Public Opinion* is an important symbol in this piece. Read it. Interview some journalism teachers, journalists and historians to understand the influence of this work on Lippmann's time and on our own time.

3) Discuss the meaning of these two sentences:

   a) "What is fine language anyway but the fabrication of future cliches?"
   b) "Surely the best kept secret of journalism is the insignificance of its subject."

4) "On the Beach" takes place in Florida. By what methods does Greenberg "bring it home" to his readers in Arkansas?

5) Greenberg talks about what it means to be addicted to writing. Have you ever had the same feeling about writing? Perhaps you have found it a plague rather than an addiction. Write an essay about your experience, good or bad, as a writer. Think back about when you first "learned" to express your ideas in writing. How did your school experiences influence the way you now approach writing? When do you feel like writing? What makes the process of writing difficult? What makes it worth doing?

Sale of a paper

APRIL 13, 1980

I have waited until the first purple martins were sighted in these latitudes to dwell on the sale of the *Delta Democrat Times* at Greenville. It was too bleak a matter to chew on before the first signs of spring in the Delta. The DDT was the late Hodding Carter's paper and for four decades and more it was a voice of reason, character, and Southern courage. It now has been sold to a chain operation for upwards of $16 million, an impressive sum even today. (Though at today's rate of inflation, it may not remain so for long.) It was a big sale, but the news of it seems less auspicious than the day Hodding Carter arrived in Greenville to start a small, struggling paper.

Having been run out of Huey Long's Louisiana for upholding certain virtues, the young editor was impressed by Greenville. As he was later to recall his first impression of its people, "They did not group their fellow townsmen in categories of wealth and poverty, success and failure, erudition and ignorance, but by the way that men and women measure up to more forthright standards. I have wondered whether these new friends were not indirectly warning us that if we too did not measure up, the new paper would not last any longer than had the levees in 1927. That does not make sense to a lot of people. A wise man shuns trouble, plays it safe, thinks of the future, waits for the draft, gets occupational exemption, and realizes that while sticks and stones may break his bones words can never hurt him. But not the broadsword clansmen of the rural South . . . ." Yes, it was the broadsword virtues that Hodding Carter upheld, and in their light the material value of his newspaper's sale seems, well, immaterial.

The growth of newspaper chains is not an unmixed curse. Some chains can improve a local paper by buying it. What may trouble in this case is the chain the DDT was sold to—Freedom Newspapers, Inc., an outfit based in Southern California whose approach is scarcely Hodding Carter's. To quote Robert Segal, president of that corporation, readers of the DDT are not likely to see many editorials in the future urging the government to champion racial equality. "We think the government should stay out of it," he said. The Carters definitely have sold the paper.

Not that their old touch had been very prominent in the DDT's pages in recent years. Hodding Carter III, once the heir apparent, is now the spokesman for the State Department's line in Washington—and, last I heard, young Hod also had signed on with the William Morris Agency. Echoing the State Department's line or showcasing one's talents strikes me, perhaps understandably, as a trifling endeavor compared to running a newspaper in a storied Southern river town. But until the sale at Greenville was announced, there was a fading hope that the DDT might be restored to its old glory in some future generation, or by an ownership more readily identifiable with Hodding Carter's convictions.

Perhaps the cruelest question about the sale put to Philip Carter was what his father would have thought about it. "I think Dad ultimately would have been enormously proud," Master Philip responded, "that a small business he helped create in a far different Mississippi had survived and thrived to the point that it could be sold for a price absolutely unheard of in the history of American newspapers. Every newspaper publisher is a businessman; what made my father extraordinary in his time was that he was a businessman with an intense social conscience. I think he would feel that much if not all of the social mission of the *Delta Democrat Times* had been fulfilled."

In the order of these brief words, old Hodding

Carter comes across as a businessman who also had certain intense convictions, rather than a man of conviction who was also in business. The more forthright standards Hodding Carter referred to may not be foremost in this talk of wealth and success and a price absolutely unheard of in the history of American newspapers. The New South has triumphed again.

"Bury the bygone South/ Bury the minstrel with the honey-mouth/ Bury the broadsword virtues of the clan," Stephen Vincent Benet sang mournfully toward the end of *John Brown's Body*. But the necessity of re-issuing a New South every 20 years or so indicates that its triumph may be fleeting. Though the broadsword virtues may be treated from time to time as picturesque accessories that have served their purpose, they may not be put down forever.

The view that much, if not all, of the old social mission now has been fulfilled is very much part of this generation's New South. Or New

America, for that matter. Behind much of the drift discernible in the news is the unstated assumption that the old challenges have been met, and most if not all of the old problems solved. The challenge of the era becomes to hold on to what our fathers wrought rather than to press ahead and take new risks, and make new sacrifices. To sum up its message: A wise man lets the past go, calls it finished, and cashes in. Perhaps that explains the sense of entropy about America behind the headlines.

It is a vanity of vanity to expect unchanging permanence in human affairs. But the earth abideth forever, and some things out to go on in a form recognizable from their past, and change only the way rivers do, to borrow another line from Stephen Vincent Benet. Things like good wines, and families, and newspapers.

Observations and questions

1) The pathetic fallacy (also discussed in the interview with Richard Zahler) is the literary notion that nature sympathizes with the feelings of man. In all three pieces, Greenberg uses nature as a symbol for his feelings and opinions. Study and discuss the methods he uses to do this. Can you think of any newspaper stories you or others have written in which a description of nature takes on symbolic significance? Don't we always use nature and weather as metaphors for our feelings as in "Don't rain on my parade"?

2) Some recurring themes in these three essays suggest they were written by the same man. They concern the meaning of history, the mutability of life, the impermanence of things, and the permanence of values. Can you think of anything else you've read that reflects these same concerns? Have you had a personal experience that inspired some of the feelings Greenberg describes? Write an essay about such an experience.

3) What kind of place is Greenville, Mississippi? What kind of place is Pine Bluff, Arkansas? Do a little research. What do the two towns have in common? What links between the two towns might make a story about Greenville interesting to a reader in Pine Bluff?

4) See if you can locate some copies of the *Delta Democrat Times* from the Hodding Carter era, or at least from the time before the paper was sold. Then get some recent editions of the paper. Examine the change in editorial philosophy. How is the change reflected in news coverage as well as editorials?

5) Consult a copy of W. David Sloan's collection *Pulitzer Prize Editorials* (Ames: Iowa State University Press, 1980). Read the editorials on race written by Southern journalists, including those by Paul Greenberg and Hodding Carter. You may want to do an essay or a research paper on the tradition of editorial writing in the South on the issue of racial justice.

A trip in time

We were driving to Little Rock to hear Orval
Faubus. Just like the old days. But Tom Parsons,
who was behind the wheel, wasn't a cub reporter
any more but managing editor. Years ago, decades ago, it had been John Thompson, the newspaper's laconic man at the legislature, who had
introduced this new editorial writer to the cock-
pit of Arkansas politics. I remember how he had
summed up Redfield on the way up to the state
Capitol: "A Faubus box." If you were limited to a
three-word description of Redfield in July of
1962, those three would be hard to beat.

But driving up this fall afternoon, everything was wrong, or anyway different. This
wasn't a snaky two-lane obstacle course but a
four-lane expressway. The most over-promised
and under-built road in the state finally had been
completed—long after Orval Faubus (who had
done most of the promising) had left the scene.
Several New Souths had come and gone since
then. The Governor's Mansion had been handed
over to a succession of Moderates and there
hadn't been a hard edge to state politics for years.

Now we were headed for Little Rock to stir
up all those old memories, and grudges. The
press had been invited to preview a television
documentary on the life and times of O. E. Faubus, Eternal Incumbent, Peerless Leader, and
footnote in American history books under Law,
Defiance of. I felt like Jack Burden in *All the
King's Men,* assigned to turn over rocks and poke
into the malice of time once more. Thus literature robs experience of its original perception, re-
placing it with somebody else's art.

And like Jack Burden toward the end of Willie Stark's saga, I wasn't looking forward to the

job. It wasn't fun any more; it was a history assignment. But when anybody begins explaining How It Really Was, somebody else needs to be around to see that the footnotes aren't misplaced. He who is allowed to control the present, as any revisionist historian knows, controls the past, and he who controls the past sways the future. History isn't just a quasi-science, and it's more than an art; it's a political weapon.

At the television station, it was like a subdued opening night, with a small bar, old friends, a comfortable board room with cushy chairs and an outsized screen on which to watch the show. And there was Orval Faubus, chatting amiably. When the hurlyburly's done, when the battle's lost and won, we'll all get together and have a drink. History, where is thy sting?

The scenes from the documentary were almost as comfortable, with a few exceptions. Like some Depression Era pictures that could have come from old WPA files. Nothing testifies to the unchanging mutability of human affairs like old photographs. But most of the documentary had the depth of a travelogue, and it came swathed in music that might have been written expressly for organists in all-you-can-eat buffeterias. It sounded both ominous and confectionary. It sounded—yes, it was—the theme from the movie *Jaws* somehow rendered toothless.

The old adrenalin didn't start to flow till well into this candy-coated production. That's when Orval Faubus up there on the screen was saying: "I think that's part of the proof that the American dream is still possible." He was talking about his own rise in politics, not his part in denying that dream to a whole race of Americans. Then the unlined Orval Faubus of 1957 was telling an incredibly young Mike Wallace in a television interview that the troops he had just called out to bar black students from Central High "will not act as segregationists or integrationists." They were there, you see, only to keep the peace. Law and order would be maintained by having the proper authorities do the mob's bidding.

As for those troops that enforced the law of the land when he wouldn't, Governor Faubus made them sound like some Foreign Legion. There he was in a newsreel of the time telling the local populace: "We are now an occupied territory." Nothing inflammatory about *his* performance in 1957.

For a brief moment, just what Orval Faubus stood for in 1957 came rushing back, along with the worldwide name he gave Arkansas that year. Then the lights came on and it was 1980 again. And one was seated next to a 70-year-old man nibbling peanuts, reminiscing about old times, and rubbing his hands together as he explained why he had retired to Houston, Texas: "I've always suffered from cold weather," this Orval Faubus was saying. Besides, he added, Houston had a lot of medical facilities. He talked of his two recent operations and the medication he took for his heart.

The old passion faded out almost as quickly as the television screen had. One recalled that in his last two times out in the gubernatorial races, Orval E. Faubus hadn't done much better than Frank Lady or Monroe Schwarzlose. He was scarcely a clear and present danger now. The second volume of his memoirs was being published by Democrat Printing & Lithographing Co. in Little Rock, which ain't exactly Harper and Row.

This Orval Faubus was repeating all the old lines, unchanged since 1957, but they no longer inspired anger. Only a certain tiredness. It is wearing to be in the presence of history's condemned, and not just because they keep repeating their brief. But because they cannot even enter a room without dragging all that irrevocable history after them, filling every space with suffocating judgment. Their unchanged routine, like an old photograph, brings home how much everything else has changed.

This Orval Faubus, for example, is still the master of the great unintended self-revelation, as when he assured those of us around the table: "I'm out of politics. I'm not running for anything. I don't have to lie to you." (Any more?) This new line may be the most revealing since the one that became the unofficial motto of his administration: Just because I said it doesn't make it so.

The sneak preview is over now, but Orval Faubus is still going strong, surrounded by reporters, rehashing old campaigns, reaching back for the names of old friends and foes. He obviously relishes it. At 70, he still enjoys the game. He will yet justify the unjustifiable, if only history would listen. He'll look better, he said, "in the perspective of history when animosities and prejudices have faded with time . . . ." It is another great quote from a politician who used animosities and prejudices so adroitly. And won six terms as governor. That seemed a long time then. Now it is the shortest, like yesterday when it is past. Stepping outside into the fresh air, I am struck again at this season by how suddenly it gets dark.

Observations and questions

1) This is an opinion piece, but it contains elements of narration. Reread "A Trip in Time" and consider how Greenberg organizes the narrative sections and blends them with commentary. Do any descriptive details contain their own commentary through implication or connotation?

2) The story assumes a certain knowledge of Orval Faubus. Read everything you can find about him. Discuss the different pictures you get of Faubus from the various works you read. Compare and contrast them to Greenberg's portrait.

3) Read *All the King's Men* by Robert Penn Warren. Also read the biography of Huey Long by T. Harry Williams and the biography of George Wallace by Marshall Frady. While you're at it, read *1984* by George Orwell and *A Clockwork Orange* by Anthony Burgess. With these in mind, write an essay considering Greenberg's statement: "History isn't just a quasi-science, and it's more than an art; it's a political weapon."

4) Some books on writing suggest that a paragraph should have unity (it is about one thing); coherence (the parts fit together); and development (it leads somewhere). Take a close look at the structure of Greenberg's paragraphs and test them against this model.

A conversation with
Paul Greenberg

CLARK: You write both unsigned editorials and signed columns. Is there a difference in your attitude, your approach, your voice in the signed vs. unsigned editorials?

GREENBERG: Yes. The signed ones are more personal. But I would like to think that they are only a trifle more personal. I don't see how I could have done the one about being on the beach as an unsigned editorial. But I would like to think that the difference is not essential on the *Pine Bluff Commercial*. I would like to think that our editorials are very personal in nature, that they don't have what is generally thought of as an institutional style. I'd like to think of the *Commercial* as a personality, so that when people say "What did the *Commercial* say about it?" they have this image of a personage speaking to them. Someone who's a hundred years old (laughs), has had many adventures, and might have acquired some experience, but is still speaking to them with a distinct voice. It's not Paul Greenberg's voice. It's the *Commercial's* voice. Now there is a certain merger, I understand. I really like the idea of calling a newspaper by the feminine pronoun, like ships and countries, because that does give it a personality.

What I sense in both your signed and unsigned editorials is a signature of style, an authentic voice of an intelligent person talking directly to me, the reader.

That's what I strive for. I really don't see why newspapers print these denatured editorials although I imagine that we too are guilty of that from time to time. But you can just pick up a newspaper and tell whether the editorial or column is speaking to you in a human voice, or if it has been programmed and is sending out editorial #742 on the welcoming of a new industry, or highway safety, or presidential endorsements.

I understand that even when you are writing on national issues you're trying to link your editorial to local concerns.

I try to link it to local references. National issues are so large that we don't have any attraction when we talk about Congress and institutions and use all the terrible words of political newspeak. If you can just reach back and use common points of reference, like Courthouse Square, or Fourth and Alabama in the heat of the day, which you share with your reader, then I think the reader gets an idea there's a human voice at the other end of the line.

Where do you get ideas for your editorials and columns?

I guess everybody has ideas for editorials. "Breathes there the editor with soul so dead/who never to himself has said/ this, this is an idea." (Laughs). I read the newspaper. I read a two-day old version of the *New York Times*. I make a point not to get it fresh. We subscribe to the *Wall Street Journal*. I get news from them and I react to them. I don't read *Time* or *U.S. News* or *Newsweek*. I would prefer to get my news unpremasticated and not at the discount store. I like book reviews. I think the *London Times Literary Supplement* is one of the great bargains in the Western World. Occasionally I read a book.

How much writing do you do?

Forty inches a day in 10-point type. Sometimes that may mean one editorial. Sometimes it may mean five or six. I write three columns a week.

But they do not all appear as signed columns in the *Commercial*. Very often I will write an editorial for the *Commercial* and then I will recast it slightly or make it more personal and it will come forth as a column which we will send to other papers.

Talk a bit about the mechanics of how you produce so much so effectively.

The stuff I like the best is the stuff that just comes pouring out. You sit down, you have a news story in front of you, and you just bang away and you get a very rough copy. But it's all there. It's probably two, three, four times as long as you want it. That may happen once or twice a year. Any other time I write from an outline. But, of course, as the piece progresses, the outline tends to change.

What does the outline look like?

It's scribbled on a yellow pad, usually about five categories, 1-2-3-4-5, maybe a subdivision under one or two, and then I begin writing. And then I look at what I have written, and I may get my scissors and slice that all up, and rearrange it. I am a very messy writer. I am never satisfied with the draft. Even after it appears in print I sometimes look over it and I think, if I had just thought to change a paragraph here or a word there, I'd be much happier. Sometimes I'll reach a point where I'll go through it and take all the commas out, and then I'll decide to put them all back in again. That's when I decide that maybe the piece is finished.

I gather that you are not working on a VDT (video display terminal).

I'm working on a typewriter. I do not think I could work very well on a VDT. I have tried it, very briefly. Perhaps I didn't give it enough of a try, but I didn't have a sense of the words. Have you run into that from anyone else?

You're the first one.

I meet these people who tell me that it's just a wonderful invention. It saves the original keystroke, and all that, and it's entirely a mystery to me.

Tell me about "On the Beach." It sounds like a Nevil Shute novel.

Yes, that's where I borrowed it. I guess the correct word would be stole (laughs). I liked the sound of the words. I don't know if I could add anything to the piece. I'm out there like a fool, with a copy of Walter Lippmann, watching the waves, and very slowly it begins to dawn on me that I ought not to be wasting my time with Walter Lippmann when I could be watching waves. I loved the waves anyway and I knew that to begin with. So it doesn't take me long to figure out which is the greater sight and more instructive. And the more lasting. And everything else follows from that.

Would you say that you are writing formal essays?

Yes, I would say it was an essay. Many of my pieces are essays.

I sense some recurring themes in these essays, themes which you rework in different ways. A theme of the impermanence of things and the permanence of certain values. Mutability and change and history.

History has always been a recurring theme of mine. I think some of these pieces were written in the fall just after my father died, and so change and mutability but also permanent values were very much with me at that time. It doesn't take much of an analyst to read that into "On the Beach." That kind of event helps you to focus on what changes and what remains. I imagine that's what you're reading into a couple of those.

Do you keep notebooks or journals?

I don't keep journals when I'm home, but I'm almost always writing when I cover something, or take a trip, or go to a press conference. The notebooks contain a series of phrases. They're not complete sentences, they're just phrases. I generally start with a phrase that strikes my ear; not my eye, my ear. Generally I have an idea that I'll be writing something about a trip. So I go through and pick out all the points that I want, so that all I'll have to do is go through and organize them, then write them out, and there it is. It's a very long, laborious process. There are long pauses in choosing the phrases you want to use, long pauses about which ones you wish to discard. Then there comes making the transitions, and finally there comes reading it over and deciding, this is a bunch of nonsense, I think I'll just write about something else. That happens with some regularity too.

Was "On the Beach" written on the spot, or was it recollected in tranquility?

Both. You can see the notes by looking at the piece. I took the weather description right out of what must have been the Pensacola newspaper because I just loved all those facts and figures and the nautical sounds. It's so different for someone from Pine Bluff. And then there's the copy of *Public Opinion,* and you have my reaction to that, and then a memory of an old joke in my head about the grandmother who wants to show you a picture of her grandchild. I wrote these down in my notebooks in very fragmented phrases that struck my ear. And then I went back to my motel room at the Holiday Inn because I had to get it down. I was writing on a yellow pad. I remember my wife disapproving. She considers that work. And then after I got back to Pine Bluff I took the rough draft, and I elaborated on some parts and I threw other parts away, and here it was.

In your essay you seem able to pull together many seemingly disparate facts and experiences into a single vision of the world.

I think I always start from some sort of emotional drive. You say that my pieces are disparate and that I bring these things together. But all these things are very familiar to me. They're part of my personality. I may be poorly integrated. But they feel familiar to me. And I have faith that if they are familiar to me, I can make them familiar to others. It's like meeting someone on a dining car of a train and he begins to tell you his life story. If he is the right kind of story teller, he may say the most outlandish things, like a Faulkner or an Isaac Bashevis Singer, and you find that rather fascinating. That is my ideal rather than my practice. I have faith that it will be of some interest to the reader and that it will all come together. I don't consider it an artificial process that I can teach someone else, but a natural one. So if I were talking to someone else I would say, "Well, you're going to have to go through your own life and find those things in it that have an emotional ring for you and integrate them into your prose."

So you see essay writing as a path to self-knowledge, as an exploration of how the mind works?

I was talking to someone at the paper the other day about the creationism controversy. And she was saying, "Why did it have to happen in Arkansas? Why did we have to be the first state when other legislatures have had the good sense to stay out of this business?" And I said: "Well, you know why it happened here. You know this is the Bible Belt. The South has had its problems integrating religion into ordinary secular affairs, unlike Puritan New England which achieved a wonderful synthesis." I got this reaction that I thought was strange and pathetic. "No, I was just born here. I'm not a Southerner." She was going to rise above it, you see, because the South had been a source of embarrassment or inconvenience to her. I think it would be very hard for her to write about these things. If people just keep their inner ear open, and look at their own experience, even though it may cause some pain, they'll be able to meet entirely strange beings, and have some interest and determination about explaining that strangeness to others. They cannot do this unless they come to terms with themselves. So I have to start with me.

Did you know what you wanted to say before you began writing "On the Beach" or did the idea come out of the writing?

I had a very clear notion, but I had an inarticulate one, if that makes any sense. I don't know how the brain works. But I had a very strong emotional feeling that did not change from the moment I conceived of "On the Beach" till I read the piece in the newspaper. The first feeling was completely wordless. The next question was to put it into words. Now I don't know the relationship between the wordless feeling and the words. I have an idea that this conversation is getting very metaphysical.

Let's talk about "A Trip in Time." I'm interested in the way you use narrative elements in your commentary. Did you continually look for opportunities to use narrative?

I'm not sure I think about it. But I often think of an essay as a story. I want to tell a story, and not just write an essay. I want the reader to say, "Yes, yes, and what happened then?"

Are you able to do that in editorials as well?

Yes, you can do that with editorials. In fact many people may not have read the original news story and may have to be clued in. Why clue them in by giving them a one paragraph summary that reads like an AP dispatch? Why not say first this happened and then this happened? In addition, you get to use your own style to describe the news event rather than one of those paragraphs filled with nouns and no verbs. The editorials I like best are ones that have some quality of moral judgment, and how do you deliver a moral without telling a story, without using the fable?

Tell me about your interest in history. I encounter more and more journalists who support their newspaper writing with a strong cultural foundation. Whether it's a love of language and literature, or a sense of history, or anthropology or mythology.

I think a newspaperman needs to have something more than a trade school background. I'm not sure he needs a trade school background if he can get the trade under his belt outside of school. He certainly needs to learn all the mechanics of the trade, but he needs an education as well. I think he needs to know one thing very well. That's been a great comfort to me. I'm very happy that I went on to graduate school and that I could see one field like American History with something more than the usual depth. It gives one confidence and at the same time a nagging doubt and a wariness about swallowing things too easily. It doesn't have to be history. It could be architecture. But a newspaperman would have a great advantage in studying art history, or the history of the feminist spirit in America, or engineering, but just something else besides trade school, be-

cause when you hear someone talk, you can realize that there is more than just what is on the
surface.

**Returning for a moment to "A Trip in Time,"
I would like to hear a bit more on how you
collected material for the beginning of that
story. There's some good reporting there,
and many editorial writers are criticized for
forgetting their reporting skills.**

I was, by the way, never a reporter. I've always
been an editorial writer. But I'm a mad note-
taker. I take more notes than I need. I was driving up to Little Rock with my old friend Tom Parsons. I was thinking about seeing Orval Faubus
who had become a kind of natural phenomenon
to me in a way, because I must have spent 75 percent of my time when I first came to the *Commercial* writing about Orval Faubus. He completely
dominated the state's political events. Going to
see a man I hadn't seen for years, naturally it
was like seeing an old friend: one dwells on
where you saw him last and what has gone since.
It's like Walker Percy's *The Moviegoer,* a kind of
natural time gauge. While sitting in Tom Par-
son's four-wheel-drive vehicle, one of the first
things that struck me was how the road had
changed. It is now a four-lane expressway. So I
wrote all these things down. I wrote many things
down that did not appear in the column. So I had
a lot of grist to work with by the time I got to Pine
Bluff.

**Let me play the cynical upstart from Long
Island for a minute. These stories are filled
with historical and literary allusions. Since
Long Islanders assume that Southerners are
simpleminded, how do you respond to the
suggestion that your audience is incapable
of understanding these references?**

How strange, because I anticipated your question as being another. I thought it would come out: How in the world would you expect anybody from Long Island to rise to understand all these local references. And I had already started to think of an answer, which was: You must under-estimate people from Long Island. If they haven't heard of certain Southernisms, they'll figure them out from context. That was not your ques-tion, but I think my answer would be essentially the same. If they have not heard of Jack Burden, or even *All the King's Men,* something tells me that they will be able to sense the allusion from the context. I have a great unreasonable faith in the power of words, and I think that if they could just be put in the proper rhythm sometimes people would understand.

Thomas Boswell
Sports Writing

THOMAS BOSWELL writes sports stories for the
Washington Post. His specialty is baseball. Boswell
joined the *Post* in 1969 as a part-time copy aide and
worked his way up to full-time sports reporter in
1972. He is 34 years old, grew up in Washington,
D.C., and was educated at Amherst College. At Amherst he studied advanced mathematics, science and
eventually became an English major. With that
checkered education he planned to enter law school,
only to be swept off his feet by the muse of sportswrit-
ing. Boswell maintains an interest in 19th century
literature, literary criticism and detective novels. In
his school days he played football and baseball, but
thanks a "bum knee" for saving him from athletic
humiliation.

Losing it
Careers fall like autumn leaves

SEPTEMBER 30, 1980

The cleanup crews come at midnight, creeping into the ghostly quarter-light of empty ballparks with their slow-sweeping brooms and languorous, sluicing hoses. All season, they remove the inanimate refuse of a game. Now, in the dwindling days of September and October, they come to collect baseball souls.

Age is the sweeper, injury his broom.

Mixed among the burst beer cups and the mustard-smeared wrappers headed for the trash heap, we find old friends who are being consigned to the dust bin of baseball's history. If a night breeze blows a back page of the Sporting News down the stadium aisle, pick it up and squint at the onetime headline names now just fine print at the very bottom of a column of averages.

Each year, the names change of those who have "lost it," and probably won't find it again. This year's list of those who are past 30 and into that inexorable stat slide includes Sal Bando, Lee May, Ed Figueroa, Gene Tenace, Fred Patek, Manny Sanguillen, Willie Horton, Bernie Carbo, Bud Harrelson, Bobby Bonds, Randy Jones, Dave Cash, Mike Torrez and Ross Grimsley. Not a bad season's haul, once you consider that, when the seine is finally culled clean, it may also hold Willie Stargell, Bill Lee and Joe Morgan.

"I like a look of Agony," wrote Emily Dickinson, "because I know it's true." For those with a taste for a true look, a glimpse beneath the mask, even if it be a glimpse of agony, then this is the proper time of year. Spring training is for hope; autumn is for reality. At every stop on the late-season baseball trail, we see that look of agony, although it hides behind many expressions.

In Pittsburgh, "Pops" Stargell rides a stationary bicycle. A depressed giant sitting on a ridiculous toy, he pedals to rehabilitate an arthritic knee that has deteriorated for a decade. "Everything gets better slower each year," he says. "And, finally, it doesn't get better at all."

In Houston, Morgan helps the Astros with the sad bits and pieces of those skills that are left to him. The back-to-back MVP, a 240-ish hitter for the past three years, says of his last career stage, "I'm still a ballplayer, but you couldn't really call me Joe Morgan . . . I'm used to laughing at other players. Now they're laughing at me."

In Montreal, "Spaceman" Bill Lee, in bullpen exile, spends these pennant-race days exorcising the nervous energy that consumes him. Lee spends half the game jogging just beyond the outfield fence, his cap and prematurely grizzled hair bouncing at the edge of view like a bobber on the water's surface being jerked about by a hooked fish. "I'm not through. They can't get rid of me," he says. "I pitched hurt for 'em for months. That explains the (bad) stats. But they don't appreciate it. Just wait. You'll see next year." It's an old litany. Lee's ERA is 5.47. Even Spacemen get jettisoned.

Finally, the towns become a swirl. The player's face is familiar with its look of wounded dignity, but the uniforms change. Jim Kaat, 41, has won 270 games, but his uniform gets harder to remember as he bounces from league to league, hanging on. "It's tough to love the game," says Kaat, now a Cardinal, "after she's stopped loving you."

To a ballplayer, the game is a seed he planted as a child, a kind of beautiful creeping ivy that he was delighted to have entwine him. As an adult, he felt supported in every sense—financial, emotional, psychic—by his green, rich, growing game, just as ivy can strengthen a brick wall. But ivy, given time, can overpower and tear down a house.

So, in a way, the aging player, whose life seems to be a mansion, knows that he is in a strong and even dangerous grip. In the end, he may not know how much of his strength, how much of his ability to stand alone, comes from the brick and mortar of his own identity and how much is borrowed from the vine that engulfs him more each year, even as it props him up. No wonder he is so fearful when the time arrives to hew through the root and pull free.

Mickey Mantle, retired a dozen years, still has a recurring dream that makes him awake in a sweat. In the nightmare, he is trying to crawl under the center field fence in Yankee Stadium, but something is snagged and he can't move. The PA system intones, "Batting fourth . . . No. 7 . . . ." In the dugout, Whitey Ford, Billy Martin and Casey Stengel ask each other, "Where's Mickey?"

"And then," says Mantle, "I wake up."

This dream needs no interpretation. It epitomizes the nub of raw, disoriented fear, and the sense of nameless loss, that many fine athletes must feel if they were ever good enough to mesh their characters with their skills. How can we tell the dancer from the dance?

Even the most dignified and self-possessed of former stars occasionally shows a twinge of what haunts Mantle. Returning from a USO tour of Korea, Marilyn Monroe told her husband, Joe DiMaggio, then retired, "Oh, Joe, it was wonderful. You never heard such cheers."

"Yes, I have," was DiMaggio's clipped reply.

The desire for applause, for camaraderie, for the hard coin of indisputable accomplishment is a powerful pull. The green of the field has so many rich connotations that it even makes the green of a dollar bill seem faded by comparison.

In all baseball history, there is perhaps only one case of a great player who cut the vine, stepped free and tested his legs long before he lost it. When Sandy Koufax was 30, he won 27 games. And after the World Series, he retired.

"I was looking for time," he now says for explanation.

Only after 13 years of casual wandering—

neither a recluse nor a public figure—did his nest egg run low. He returned to baseball, as a Dodger coach, because it was a painless way to make a buck as a pitching professor emeritus.

Koufax is simply the exception that proves the rule. Far more typical are Hank Aaron and Warren Spahn, the top home run hitter and winner in modern, lively-ball times. The former Brave teammates never faced each other in their careers, but they did this spring in San Diego when the 46-year-old Aaron came to bat against the 59-year-old Spahn. They weren't kidding.

Not since Babe Ruth faced Walter Johnson for charity when both were in their 50s have such legends met. The pretext for this time-warp freeze frame was a Padre-vs.-Pirate home run-hitting contest. But the real curiosity was watching Aaron and Spahn face each other from opposite ends of the tunnel of middle age. Aaron looked like he had spent his four retirement years locked in a bakery. Spahn might have spent 15 years prospecting in a desert, his skin weathered to rawhide, his bandy limbs and barrel chest shrunken.

The scene was elegantly set. Warming up, Aaron missed half-speed pitches. The crowd murmured its collective embarrassment and empathy as though an innocent prank had turned ugly. Meanwhile, thanks to aluminum bats and Japanese rabbit balls, Dave Parker, Dave Winfield and Stargell were having a tape-measure orgy. Aaron was mercifully forgotten.

Once the contest started, Aaron whiffed meekly twice against the Padre batting practice pitcher. Then, on the third of six allotted swings in the round, Aaron conked a homer. The crowd cheered with relief. Then, while their pitying applause was still in the air, the next pitch had already been dispatched even further into the left field bleachers. The crowd was rising and roaring. Reporters scrambled back into the press box just as players popped back out of runways into the dugouts to watch. The next pitch also went over the wall, delivered there by a sweet slash of the wrists. And, on his fourth consecutive swing—all this in 30 seconds or so, as emotions had gone from depression to glee—Aaron smashed his last pitch off the top of the center field wall 430 feet away, missing a fourth homer by a yard.

For the final round of the contest, Spahn pitched, lobbing in mush balls for the monsters to mash. Aaron hit last, needing just one homer to beat all the active stars. Spahn peered in, grinned and threw. Aaron swung and missed. He smiled back at Spahn. Spahn repeated the ritual and threw again. Aaron looked at the pitch as though it were a rotten mackerel. Although he was due five more swings, Aaron gently laid down his bat, turned his back on Spahn and walked away, ending the contest by fiat.

Back in the dugout, Aaron was asked, "Why'd you quit? Hurt yourself swinging?"

"No," said Aaron brusquely. "Spahn was

throwing screwballs."

And they say Walter Johnson threw sliders to Ruth.

In baseball, you see, no one ever believes he's really lost it. No American team sport is half so fascinated with the process of aging as baseball, perhaps because none of our games is so based on skill and timing rather than brute force. Nor does any sport offer prospects for an athletic old age that is so rich in possibilities for either humiliation or the greatest fame.

Every athlete in every sport deteriorates. But in baseball that battle against time—where a standoff means temporary victory—can be extended for as much as a decade by a dogged will and an analytical mind. Perhaps no sport encourages its men to rage so nobly against the erosion of their youth.

The ultimate cases in point are Aaron and Spahn, statistically the greatest old hitter and the best old pitcher ever. They alone among Hall of Famers actually got better after they turned 35. Aaron hit 245 homers and had his two best slugging-percentage years after that supposed watershed as he actually became a better pull hitter with age. After Spahn turned 35, and concurrently mastered the scroogie, he won 20 games seven times and won 180 games. No one is close to either mark.

Baseball, it seems, rewards stubbornness and indomitability, as long as those qualities are mixed with a basic humility, self-knowledge and willingness to adapt. Baseball's highest, and most appealing, type may be the veteran. No sport is so full of 10-, 15- and even 20-year pros, or is so defined by them.

"I disagree," John Keats once wrote in a letter, about the world as a "vale of tears . . . . Call the world, if you please, 'the vale of soul-making.' Then you will find out the use of the world."

Only with age do athletes discover that their playing fields have become vales of soul-making. Only as they become vulnerable, flawed and afraid do they seem truly human to us and most worthy of our attention. Nothing can stop the slow bleeding away of talent and confidence, but character is the best tourniquet.

"The player who ages poorly is the one who lets his vanity get in the way of his judgment," says Yankee Coach Charlie Lau. "Making 'adjustments' is another word for having the good sense to know you're getting older."

As an example, Lau cites those good friends, George Scott and Reggie Jackson. Each, with age, showed a hitting flaw. Scott, proud of his strength, could no longer manage his huge 38-ounce bat. Jackson had trouble with high and outside fast balls, popping them harmlessly to center. Scott, for three years, refused to use a lighter bat. Despite humiliating reverse shifts—with defenses playing him as though he were a weak lefty hitter—he persisted in his persona as "The Boomer." Now, he's out of baseball and doesn't understand. Jackson, on the other hand, worked with his stance and weight shift until that troublesome pitch suddenly became his bleacher meat. Now, at 34, he has his highest homer total since he was 23.

"Even after everybody else told Scott he needed to change, he wouldn't," summarized Lau. "But before anybody said anything to Reggie, he already had."

No better text could be asked to illustrate baseball's capacity for allowing age-with-dignity than the performance in the past month of the New York Yankees. Of all champions, they may well be the oldest, the most infirm and the most emblematic of what we mean by veteran fortitude.

If ever a team ought not bear inspection, it is these Yankees with a pitching rotation of Gaylord Perry (42), Luis Tiant (40), Tommy John (37) and Rudy May (37). Yet they are 20-3 in September. Autumn must be their proper season. More than half this team has, at one time or another, heard the words, "You've lost it." Names like Piniella, Nettles, Jackson, Watson, Murcer, Spencer, Rodriguez and Stanley have, among them, an average age of 35.

Look below the Yankee dollar signs and New York headlines. This is a team familiar with the look of Agony. Its players have been forced to look in the mirror. For most, their baseball world long ago became a vale of soul-making.

So, demands for September character have been within their reach. When the cleanup crews come to sweep out darkened Yankee Stadium this year, there will be no human refuse. All those aged expendables who were management's list for replacement with shiny expensive new parts have, by banding together, made themselves indispensable for at least a few months.

Age, with his broom of injury, will sweep them out someday. But, until then, these Yankees are a standing lesson of how old men, who are really young, can staunchly refuse to go gentle into that good night.

Observations and questions

1) Tone is a key element in this story. How does Boswell use language in the first three paragraphs to evoke feelings of nostalgia in his readers? Consider the rhythms of the sentences, the imagery and the scene.

2) In his introduction, Boswell creates a "conceit," or extended metaphor, that compares age to a sweeper. Think of some other symbols for age, death and the ravages of time. How appropriate is Boswell's image?

3) There is a literary feeling about this piece, not only because of Boswell's elegant style, but because of specific literary allusions. He quotes a poem from Emily Dickinson and a letter of John Keats. Is Boswell's audience sophisticated enough to make sense of these allusions? Find the sources of these allusions, read them, and examine their application by Boswell.

4) Did you recognize the final lines of the story as an allusion to the Dylan Thomas poem "Do not go gentle into that good night"? Read the poem and discuss why Boswell decided to use it.

5) We always look for timeliness in journalism, even in a set piece like this one. What elements in Boswell's story make it relevant to the news of the day? Has he done enough to emphasize these elements?

6) This story hangs on a line of anecdotes about aging stars: Mantle, DiMaggio, Spahn and Aaron. Examine each anecdote and discuss why Boswell places it where it is.

7) Throughout, Boswell touches on the symbolic elements of baseball: "The green of the field has so many rich connotations . . . ." What are some of these connotations?

8) George Orwell says a writer should ask these questions: "What am I trying to say? What words will express it? What image or idiom will make it clearer?" Consider the images that Boswell uses throughout. How do they enhance our understanding in the story:

> "To a ballplayer, the game is a seed he planted as a child."
> The image of the ivy vines.
> The physical descriptions of Spahn and Aaron.

9) Isn't this a rather off-beat story? Do you imagine seeing it in many newspapers? Most sports sections stick to game stories and player profiles. Think of 10 story ideas that relate to the world of sports but which would be unusual to see on most sports pages.

The FIGHT

MONTREAL — Boxing at its best is beastly.

If that assumption holds no appeal, then you cannot relish the stirring and horrid spectacle of Roberto Duran's public assault on Sugar Ray Leonard here on Friday.

Boxing is about pain. It is a night out for the carnivore in us, the hidden beast who is hungry.

Few men have ever become world champion without facing that dark side of their game; Leonard was one.

Leonard might even have arrived in this cosmopolitan city to defend his WBC welterweight crown still believing, at 24, that his profession was a sport rather than a disturbing, paradoxical arena where vice and virtue sometimes exchange roles once they enter the ring.

Duran, who has been the quintessential creature of the ring in his time, acquainted Leonard with the true facts about his business.

After a lifetime of hard work but almost effortless success inside the ropes, Leonard finally came face to face with the core of boxing: suffering. He passed the test of personal courage but, because he was so intent on that examination of character, he neglected the tactics of his art and lost a crown.

Someday, if the '80s turns out to be a decade of Leonard evolution, this fight—called *"le face a face historique"*—may prove to be historic because it brought a great young fighter face to face with fear.

Duran, only the third man ever to be both lightweight and welterweight champion, won a unanimous decision over Leonard by a slim and controversial margin.

Leonard won a unanimous and incontrovertible decision over fear. This defeat was his letter of credit to a doubting world that thought him a likeable boxer, but not necessarily a heroic fighter.

Few fights in history, certainly very few in the last 20 years, have met boxing's highest and most dubious standard of greatness: the constant, relentless and mutual inflicting of the maximum tolerable amount of pain.

By that measure, the Leonard-Duran conflagration was worth every penny of the $30 million that it probably will gross. No one who is fascinated by watching men under extreme duress was cheated.

Duran, given his choice, would fight 15 rounds in a telephone booth without any intermissions. Only the Panamanian brawler, among current fighters, can monopolize 399 square feet of a 400-square-foot ring. Duran's victims sometimes wonder if they have room to fall.

That was the case for the first five and last five rounds of Friday night's classic, which was as riveting as boxing can be without knockdowns or copious blood.

Experts will argue interminably over why Leonard fought what appeared to be a brave but hopelessly stupid fight. Why didn't he jab? Why didn't he dance? Why didn't he circle? Why didn't he slide when Duran tried to cut the ring? Why didn't he clinch or push off more to avoid the infighting? Why did he stand toe to toe countless times and exchange hooks to the head and uppercut digs to the gut?

Only Leonard had the absolute and unarguable answer.

"I had no other alternative," he said.

Early in the fight, when Duran was fresh, and late in the fight, when Leonard was tired, Duran made certain that the fight would be conducted only one way—his way.

Wherever Leonard was, there was Duran—less than arm's reach away and throwing leather without surcease. In such circumstance, no man can dance, or jab or slide. Once Duran is within the parameters of an opponent's defense, and both his hands of stone are moving, a fighter has only one choice: exchange punches or call for mama.

• • •

The tone of a brutal and elemental evening was established quickly when prelim lightweight Cleveland Denny was carried out unconscious in convulsive paroxysms so strong that doctors could not get the mouthpiece out of his clenched jaw. Denny is in intensive care.

For any in the crowd of 46,317—the once-a-year boxing fans like Jack Nicklaus—who might doubt, that twitching body on the stretcher was a declaration of boxing's basic nature.

When Gaetan Hart, the man who knocked out Denny, was told that his last punch hardly seemed powerful enough for such damage, he was offended. His last opponent left the ring in a coma and required eight hours of brain surgery, so Hart, with his matted hair, tattoos and rearranged features, is proud of his punch. In this life, it is what he has.

"When I hit Denny with the right hand," explained Hart, "his eyes go around backwards like this."

And Hart twirled his forefingers as though illustrating how the cherries on a slot machine revolve.

That is boxing. And Duran, the man who, in the ring, has the hands and the heart of stone, knows it better than any fighter of his generation.

Other boxing eras would not have found Duran unique. His personality type would have seemed comfortably familiar: a fatherless street urchin who stole to feed his brothers and sisters, dropped out of school in the third grade at the age of 13, turned pro at 16, became the athletic pet of a Latin military dictator, won a world title at age 21, and now has a fleet of gaudy cars and a 680-pound pet lion which he walks on a leash.

In any period, Duran would have stood out. But in the '60s and '70s, when Muhammad Ali brought footwork, defense, an unmarked face and poetry to fighting, Duran seemed almost an embarrassing anachronism, a stage in boxing's evolution that the game seemed anxious to act as though it had passed.

Duran, with his 71-1 record, seldom got his due. Or if he did, it was done with a shudder as though Heathcliff were being introduced in polite society and might smash the china in a rage.

But boxing never changes. One central truth lies at its heart and it never alters: pain is the most powerful and tangible force in life.

The threat of torture, for instance, is stronger than the threat of death. Execution can be faced, but pain is corrosive, like an acid eating at the personality.

Pain, as anyone with a toothache knows, drives out all other emotions and sensations before it. Pain is priority. It may even be man's strongest and most undeniable reality.

And that is why the fight game stirs us, even as it repels us.

· · ·

For at least 10 of their 15 rounds, Leonard and Duran set as intense a pace as any fan could wish—they looked like Ali and Smokin' Joe Frazier in the first round in Manila but, because they weigh only 147 pounds, their speed and frequency of violence did not dwindle nearly so much as the fight wore on.

"He threw his best, I threw my best," said Leonard.

What landed? he was asked.

"Everything," said Leonard.

In the early rounds, there was defense, slipping and blocking of the fiercest punches. In the late rounds, when the blows still carried pain but insufficient force for a blessed unconsciousness, every third swing seemed to land flush.

Only in the middle rounds, starting late in the fifth, when Leonard finally landed enough consecutive punches to make Duran back off for the first time, and extending through the 10th, did Leonard achieve a painless *modus vivendi*.

Then, Leonard still had his speed and Duran had his doubts. The Sugar Man struck and escaped, dealt fire for fire, then had breathing time to regroup.

After those early rounds of perplexity bordering on fear, Leonard gradually gained confidence—more's the pity for him—until, by the 11th, he thought he was Duran's better. He thought he could reach into the furnace and save the crown that he saw melting there.

That 11th round was meant for the film archives. Everything that gives boxing undeniable dimension and emotional authority was wrought to white heat then.

Money, glory or the search for identity may get a man into the ring, but only facing and surmounting pain can keep him there. Only that act of creating a brutal art in the presence of suffer-

ing can bring nobility to man's oldest and most visceral competition.

Boxing has the cleanest line, the fewest rules and the most self-evident objective of any endeavor that people gather to watch.

When shabbily done, like the third meeting of their careers between Denny and Hart—a pair of lifelong plodders—few things are so worthless and destructive. Life and death on the undercard is as depressing as the sporting life gets.

However, at certain heights of skill and will, fighters like Duran and Leonard begin to carry with them a symbolic nimbus. They seem a distillation of their backgrounds, their time and place and the people out of which they sprang.

Only when Duran is seen in this way does that 11th round, and what he did after it, seem inevitable.

Here in Montreal, this town of boutiques and glass-and-neon malls where an obsession with the latest imported European fashion is everywhere, Duran's fans and followers have looked as alien as Martians.

In swanky hotels like the Meridien, the Regency and the Bonaventure, these people who chant "Cholo"—the word for a Panamanian of Indian descent—and talk constantly with animated delight are distinguished by more than their old, clean, one-suit-per-lifetime clothes.

Their hands and faces, like Duran's, have been weathered by eternal forces—the erosion of work, age and the rub of stubborn necessities.

In Olympic Stadium on a cool Canadian night, with salsa music in the upper deck, Duran's people—his true kin or those here who have adopted him—cheered with raw conviction.

Out of our pestilential sump holes of social unconsciousness rise up a few strong, if lopsided personalities, who create much of our public collective mythology. Duran is a sample of that up-from-under caste that seems simple, unified and forceful.

In the 11th, that absence of complexity proved useful.

Leonard had mustered both his confidence and his resolve.

"Sugar Ray is like the rain," said Leonard's sparring partner Mike James before the fight. "Once he gets started, you can't make him stop."

Leonard had clouded up and was in full thunderclap. Just as Duran had had Leonard deeply worried and near trouble in his second-round blitz, Leonard now was sure he was going for a kill. "I hit Duran some tremendous shots with left hooks, right hooks and overhand rights," said Leonard.

Instead of covering up, Duran met the pain directly, almost welcomed it. The more his head was battered from side to side, the more his fists flew in return. By midround, Leonard was so arm weary from punching that his gloves slipped to his waist. Duran took the initiative in the assault and battering until, by round's end, Leonard was in another desperate retaliatory rage, storming down punches on Duran after the bell sounded.

The net effect of this sustained firestorm was not a new balance of terror, but merely a change in exhaustion levels. Leonard had gambled and lost. The fight reverted to its early-round syndrome with Duran boring inside against a game but stationary Leonard.

Had Leonard resisted the impulse to knock out his taunter, had he stayed with his midround style as long as his energy lasted, those ever-so-close judges' cards (146-144, 145-144 and 148-147) might have been reversed.

• • •

It is appropriate that in such a morally ambiguous sport, one of boxing's great fights should leave behind it a mood of nagging paradox.

A view of the world—usually unspoken—often hangs around the edges of major sports. Certainly it always has with boxing.

The notion that life is a fight is inescapable

in this subculture of leather and liniment. The search for glory through taking advantage, the constant pursuit of getting the better of someone are precepts so ingrained that no one would think to preach them.

As a consequence, those who tend to see the world that way are drawn here: politicians, mobsters, business millionaires, junkies of all persuasions, entertainers, athletes and journalists.

It is a night for those who have sharp teeth, or think they do; vegetarians and saints need not apply.

However, this shark ethic may have been carried further—reduced really to the absurd— in boxing than in any other corner of our culture. The big eating the little is gospel.

That is why Leonard entered this scene as such a refreshing anomaly. Essentially, he was a world champion who had none of boxing's shabby back-room entanglements.

It was no accident that this fight could gross more money ($30 million predicted) and bring more to the fighters themselves (at least $8 million to Leonard and $1.5 million to Duran) than any fight in history.

Leonard's lawyer, Mike Trainer, set a precedent of squeezing out middle-men and promoters, keeping the financial books above board and making no private deals.

But as soon as this beastly good fight ended, the big sharks of boxing began circling.

Duran, as devoid of *duende*—that indefinable Latin mixture of style and class—out of the ring as he is chocked with it inside the ropes, sat beside his boxing godfather Don King, the promoter.

As Duran attacked an orange—spitting seeds and rind in any direction as he held a surly, gloating, graceless press conference—King, his hair electrified and his vanity in full bloom, took out a huge roll of big bills.

With great pretense, King began slapping the money in Duran's palm of stone as the photographers clicked.

Not only Sugar Ray Leonard had been beaten, but Sugar Ray Leonard Inc., too. That great perennial enemy of boxing—an honest fighter—had been removed from the game's top rung.

And that, on one of boxing's best nights, was a beastly development, indeed.

Observations and questions

1) If there were no byline on "Losing It" or "The Fight," what evidence would there be that they were written by the same person? Is there a signature of style that identifies the author?

2) Consider Boswell's description of Duran fighting in a telephone booth. Imitating that passage, describe the styles of other athletes you may know: Muhammad Ali, George Brett, Reggie Jackson, Lynn Swann, Julius Erving.

3) Describe how Boswell moves back and forth between abstract concepts (heroism, suffering) to concrete events and scenes.

4) An important subplot in this piece concerns the Hart-Denny fight. How does Boswell use the two fights to reflect his own ambivalence about boxing?

5) The 11th round is the key round in the fight. How does Boswell lead up to it and move away from it?

6) We all know that reporters have feelings, even if the cinematic stereotype suggests otherwise. What are Boswell's feelings about boxing? How does he manifest them? Are you upset that he does not seem objective? Examine your own feelings about boxing. Write them down.

7) Read Norman Mailer's essay "The Death of Benny Paret." Paret was a fighter who was beaten to death in the ring. Mailer watched the fight and wrote about the surrounding controversy. Contrast the styles of the two writers.

Phillies end century of frustration

OCTOBER 21, 1980

PHILADELPHIA — The Philadelphia Phillies' life passed before their eyes tonight. All 97 years of it.

In the eighth and ninth innings of this sixth and final game of the World Series, the Phillies not only had to beat the Kansas City Royals, 4-1, they had to defeat their own history and re-nounce a century of baseball antitradition.

Who says that you cannot live down the past—that man, by his deeds, cannot create a re-birth of his own dignity? Philadelphia—the city that played and of course lost the first game in the annals of the National League in 1876—won its first world championship tonight in delirious, barely believing Veterans Stadium.

The heartbreak Phillies, the franchise born to failure in 1883 and firmly entrenched as base-ball's 97-year weaklings ever since, went down twice tonight as though they were drowning. Twice, as the Royals loaded the bases, every true Phillie fan had to think of his decades of sadness. Fifty-one seasons in the Baker Bowl and nary a Series win. Thirty-two years in Shibe Park, later Connie Mack Stadium, and nothing in the way of diamond-centered rings.

Those buildings, which lasted longer than the lives of many men, are torn down now. That is how you measure real failure—not in seasons, but in buildings crumbled down under the weight of defeat. And now, 10 more seasons in the Vet, perhaps the most painful of all because of the playoff flops of '76, '77 and '78. In each of those final two innings this night of redemption, Royals danced off every base as little exhausted Tug McGraw, so frazzled that he almost begged his manager to take him off the mound, battled the best hitting team in 30 years with just one pitch—his nothing ball. It was McGraw, as a New York Met, who said, "You gotta believe." Such words would seem foreign in a Phillie's mouth. When the bases were jammed with blue-clad Royals this night, their names might as well have been Failure, Frustration and Lost Faith.

When McGraw got Kansas City cleanup man Hal McRae to ground to second base to end the eighth, it was a punch in the teeth to that trio of dark Phillie Phates. When Pete Rose made a miraculous knee-high reflex grab of a foul pop after it popped out of catcher Bob Boone's glove on the lip of the Phillie dugout for the second out of the ninth, nearly every soul of the 65,838 in this park began to feel a tingle. Rose, symbol of victory and of indomitability, is the emblem of the new, blessedly forgetful Phillies—the team that wouldn't die.

This time, the Phils didn't go down for the third time. When McGraw finally struck out Willie Wilson—the indisputable goat of this Series—in the ninth, the Phillies, and all who have stayed with them throughout the most troubled of baseball love affairs, burst through to the surface and gulped the fresh air.

The long, long bad dream was over. In a scene as ambiguous, prickly and hard to embrace as this Phillie team, the new champions screamed and hugged on a field encircled by police dogs, police horses, helmeted guards as numberless as Phillie defeats. Anybody who wanted to kiss this team would have to get billy clubbed to do it.

The final score of this game is so deceitful. Years from now, who will guess that a 4-1 lead could feel like less than one run? Few fans will remember how the Phillies built their 4-0 lead. Mike Schmidt, the Series MVP with his seven RBI, got the game-winning, bases-loaded, two-run single to right field way back in the fourth inning to knock out starter Rich Gale, who only got six outs. In the fifth, it was Bake McBride scoring

Lonnie Smith from third with a one-out grounder to short for an insurance run. And in the sixth, Larry Bowa doubled and Bob Boone scored him with a rifle single to left for a 4-0 lead.

Never did a four-run margin seem so superfluous or prove so necessary. The winner, Steve Carlton, worked seven of the most overpowering innings imaginable, a four-hit, seven-strikeout performance worthy of the legendary Lefty, the man with more strikeouts than any southpaw in history.

But in the eighth, those bad memories, those Phillie nightmares began. After a walk and single with no outs, Manager Dallas Green relieved Carlton after his 109th pitch. In retrospect, it was probably a blunder worthy of Phillie skippers such as Gavvy Cravath, Wild Bill Donovan or Kaiser Wilhelm. Or Danny Ozark. Carlton was great, but tiring. McGraw was exhausted from his first pitch. McGraw bounced curves. He threw fast balls head high. Nobody would chase his screwball. He was in a world of trouble and he knew it.

"I kept getting in trouble, falling behind hitters, so I had to come in with a fat pitch. I kept telling myself, 'Use your fielders,' " said McGraw, who has pitched in nine of the Phillie 11 postseason games. "I felt somewhat in control of the inning in the eighth. But, after the first hitter in the ninth, my arm got really tired." Anybody's arm would be tired with 97 years worth of ghosts sitting on it.

The first hint of drama, of possible Phillie disaster, came on McGraw's second batter. He started by getting hopeless Frank White (two for 25) to foul out to Rose. But when he walked the ineffectual Wilson to load the bases with one out, it was obvious that McGraw was laboring worse than the man he'd replaced. McGraw got U.L. Washington to hit a meaningless sacrifice fly to center field for the second out.

However, even as the only K.C. run was sprinting home, all eyes were on George Brett, the tie run stepping up. McGraw, the only pitcher of '80 to fan Brett on consecutive at bats when they met on Sunday, had a triumph, of sorts. Brett only hit a rocket in the hole toward right field. It should have been a clean hit, but Manny Trillo, with the range of radar, sped left, then threw to first in time to beat Brett.

That is, if Rose hadn't gotten his feet tangled, stumbled over the bag, and missed tagging it by an inch. That's when this became the World Series. Had Pete Rose, in his old age, become a cursed and bedeviled Phillie, too?

When McRae, who stepped up with a career average of .450 in three Series, fouled off three full-count pitches, with all runners blazing, this park was drained of emotion. His routine ground ball to Trillo seemed like a blessed dispensation. Surely, that was the last test.

Never for the Phillies.

McGraw's whiff of Amos Otis to start the ninth was illusion. The truth began to show when Willie Aikens walked and two sad Series hitters, Duke Wathan and Jose Cardenal, ripped singles to right and to center to load the bases.

Nobody had the least doubt. McGraw had nothing. Nothing but the one thing Phillies aren't supposed to have. "The only reason it's impossible to hate the Phillies' guts," the saying goes here, "is because they don't have any."

McGraw had plenty. Maybe he couldn't overpower, but he could change speeds. He could prey on overanxiousness.

To the Phils' eternal great good luck, the two last Royals batters were the worst—White and Wilson (four for 26). They had ghosts, too. The worst kind. Not team ghosts, but personal ghosts. White was a desperate man. He swung at the first pitch for the second consecutive time against McGraw and popped it up foul for the second time. Boone drifted over. Plenty of time. Nice easy squeeze . . . oooops!

It happened almost too fast for the eyes, this play that may have saved a Series game, even

saved a world championship since the Phils might well have unraveled had they lost tonight.

Rose stood a yard from Boone, overseeing the Phillies' fate, as is his wont. In a tenth of a second, Rose earned all of the $3.2 million he is being paid for four seasons here. His glove flicked out, quick as a lizard gobbling a fly, and snatched the ball just as it was about to plop symbolically into the Phillies' laps.

Every Royal heart must have sunk as Wilson stepped to the plate. He threw in the towel long ago, flipping his hat and bat away in resigned, limp disgust after Carlton struck him out twice tonight. Wilson's final strikeout, chasing a shoulder-high fast ball, was his 12th strikeout of this Series—a record. In all 77 Classics, it is possible that no player ever came into a Series with such mammoth numbers (.326, 230 hits, 79 steals) and was so completely eaten alive by October pressure.

And, perhaps, the right man to capture this

160

night was team president Ruly Carpenter, a sec-
ond-generation owner who has spent his life im-
mersed in trying to overcome invisible enemies.

Soaked with champagne, he rode back up to
the Phillies' offices in a tiny elevator. How do you
feel? he was asked.

"Fine," said Carpenter, numb for the moment. Then his face came alive, he smiled, the re-
alization of victory growing.

"Finally," he said.

KANSAS CITY	ab	r	h	bi	PHILADELPHIA	ab	r	h	bi
Wilson lf	4	0	0	0	L. Smith lf	4	2	1	0
Wshngtn ss	3	0	1	1	Gross lf	0	0	0	0
G. Brett 3b	4	0	2	0	Rose 1b	4	0	3	0
McRae dh	4	0	0	0	Schmidt 3b	3	0	1	2
Otis cf	3	0	0	0	McBride rf	4	0	0	1
Aikens 1b	2	0	0	0	Luzinski dh	4	0	0	0
Cncpcion pr	0	0	0	0	Maddox cf	4	0	2	0
Wathan c	3	1	2	0	Trillo 2b	4	0	0	0
Cardenal rf	4	0	2	0	Bowa ss	4	1	1	0
White 2b	4	0	0	0	Boone c	2	1	1	1
Total	31	1	7	1	Total	33	4	9	4

Kansas City	000	000	010—1
Philadelphia	002	011	00x—4

E—White, Aikens, DP—Kansas City 1,
Philadelphia 2. LOB—Kansas City 9,
Philadelphia 7. 2B—GMaddox, L Smith,
Bowa. SF—Washington.

ROYALS PITCHING

	IP	H	R	ER	BB	SO
Gale L,0-1	2	4	2	1	1	1
Martin	2⅓	1	1	1	1	0
Splittorff	1⅔	4	1	1	0	0
Pattin	1	0	0	0	0	2
Quisenberry	1	0	0	0	0	0

PHILLIES PITCHING

	IP	H	R	ER	BB	SO
Carlton W, 2-0	7	4	1	1	3	7
McGraw S,2	2	3	0	0	2	2

Gale pitched to four batters in third.
Splittorff pitched to one batter in seventh
Carlton pitched to two batters in eighth.
T—3:00.   A—65,838

Observations and questions

1) Most people agree that great sportswriters have helped evolve the mythology and folklore of sports. Probably the greatest—and most over-written—lead of all time is Grantland Rice's rendition of the 1924 Notre Dame-Army football game:

"Outlined against a blue-gray October sky, the Four Horsemen rode again. In dramatic lore they are known as Famine, Pestilence, Destruction and Death. These are only aliases. Their real names are Stuhldreher, Miller, Crowley and Layden. They formed the crest of the South Bend cyclone before which another fighting Army football team was swept over the precipice at the Polo Grounds yesterday afternoon as 55,000 peered down on the bewildering panorama spread on the green plain below."

That passage, purple as it is, turned a football team into a legend. Is Boswell doing the same sort of thing—in a much more lighthearted way—in his description of the Phillie Phates: Failure, Frustration, and Lost Faith? What role does hyperbole—rhetorical exaggeration—play in all of Boswell's pieces? Do you agree, for example, that Pete Rose earned his $3.2 million by snagging a single pop fly? Consider the larger question of how baseball, and sports in general, functions as an important American cultural myth.

2) This is primarily a game story. Yet Boswell fills it with baseball lore, history and tradition. Examine the structure of the piece, then describe how Boswell combines background information with news about the game.

3) Does this story assume the reader has a certain knowledge of baseball? What assumption is Boswell making about the reader? Show this piece to someone who knows nothing about baseball. What is that person's reaction? Now show it to an expert on baseball. Most editors think it is important for, say, a government writer to translate jargon for his readers. Do we make the same demands of sportswriters?

A conversation with
Thomas Boswell

(Thomas Boswell was interviewed by telephone from the Augusta National Golf Club where he was covering the Masters Tournament.)

CLARK: In college you studied advanced mathematics, science, and literature. You were considering law. What led you to journalism?

BOSWELL: I always wanted to find out if I could write, and I always assumed that the biggest problem for a writer was to find some way to exist until he had some experience to write about. What do you do? I have so many friends who went to Majorca to write an epic poem when they were 23. I have friends who were cabdrivers in New York, or who lived in a kibbutz in Israel, friends who are scattered over various continents who thought they were writers.

So you weren't about to sing the blues, in other words.

(Laughs.) I wasn't going to sing the blues or pay my dues. And I wasn't going to write at the whim of some muse that may not exist. I wanted to sit down and face the blank sheet of paper every day. I thought newspaper writing was a way to overcome that enormous block of facing your own writing.

Have you ever faced the "toytown syndrome" as a sportswriter? You know, the notion that the sports department is just playland, not concerned with serious topics?

There's a nice book called *The Joy of Sports* written by a first-rate theologian, Michael Novak, that's ambitious in the opposite direction. But I do think that sports writers are dealing with mythical and anthropological subjects. I do think it's a distinct step down to write for any other section of the paper than the sports section.

I can see mythical and anthropological elements in all three of your stories.

When you fly over Cincinnati or Pittsburgh, the biggest things in those cities are the stadiums. The place in many major cities where you draw the biggest, the most enthusiastic, the most emotional crowds, are sporting events. Something's happening there. I think it's one of the few places that we talk about mythological stories. Society is very weak on religion now. When people want to express their values, quite often sports is the metaphor that they use for talking about more serious subjects.

Some would argue, Tom, that sports have changed so much since we were children. I used to worship Mickey Mantle. Is that kind of idealism possible today? Don't you think that things have changed?

Only to make it more interesting. I think our heroes are as largely drawn as ever. I'm not a debunker. My hero could have been Roy Sievers. Somebody else's hero in my area could be Eddie Murray or Ken Singleton. The fact that they have a symbolic quality shouldn't obscure the fact that you deal with them only as people. There seems to be a problem for a lot of writers. They're either looking up at athletes, or they're looking down at them. I don't understand why you can't look them in the eye.

So you have no trouble dealing with athletes?

I never wanted to grow up to be an athlete. I wanted to grow up to be a writer. And one of the things that makes them good subjects is that many athletes are still in touch with rather basic emotions. Most people may be 40 or 50 before they deal with the basic things in their lives. I think athletes have an accelerated maturation process. It's hard to find a 23-year-old athlete who doesn't seem to be 33, or a 28-year-old athlete who doesn't seem to be 40. People say they're protracted adolescents. I don't find that at all. They're more mature, with a greater sense of themselves, of a lifework, even if it is only a game. They sense that that lifework is very fleeting. They can't afford to be rookies more than one year. In other walks of life you feel you're a rookie for five years or 10 years.

When you go to the American Press Institute to talk to journalists about writing, what do you tell them?

I tell them that I think all stories fall into the same three categories as Shakespeare's: comedies, tragedies and histories. When you're writing a game story, or an account of the labor negotiations in baseball, you're writing instant history. There are many times when you can be writing comedy. I wrote a piece for today's *Post* about the great hullabaloo in Augusta where the sacred Augusta greens were torn up and replaced with another type of grass and how this has sent the entire golf community into a collective emotional breakdown. And certainly there are tragedies. I see stories falling into those categories. I don't say I'm writing a feature story or a news lead. I never see things that way.

Tell me about the mechanics of your writing.

Basically simple things. I think writing is rewriting. I love the new computer terminals. Instead of writing the first six paragraphs 10 or 12 times

— when you do that you've literally typed 70 to 100 paragraphs which is physically hard. It wastes an enormous amount of energy. With the new computer terminals you can really play with things. It's improved my speed so much that it's amazing to me. The more you're addicted to rewriting, the nicer those computers are.

Do you begin with an outline, or do you sit down and write as fast as you can?

When I was in college, I believed that inspiration sat on your shoulder. I think that a lot less now. The most important thing in the story is finding the central idea. It's one thing to be given a topic, but you have to find the idea or the concept within that topic. Once you find that idea or thread, all the other anecdotes, illustrations and quotes are pearls that you hang on this thread. The thread may seem very humble, the pearls may seem very flashy, but it's still the thread that makes the necklace.

You find that thread through the process of writing, or do you need it before you begin to write?

While you're interviewing you're looking for it. After I've done all my interviewing, I often still have no idea what the story is. Sometimes it doesn't come to you until you're actually writing the piece. Then you say: Oh, I see what I'm talking about, I knew there was something here. And then maybe you have to go back and start rewriting.

And you just stick with it until you find it.

When you're writing it's important to keep your feet still. There's too much desire to walk around the room, avoid the story, to try to find a wonderful outline, to go back and reresearch things for the 85th time, to fill out file cards — all because

you don't want to face the actual task of writing.
Sometimes you simply have to put your feet
down and start writing. And maybe in your 8th
or 10th or 15th paragraph you'll stumble onto
your lead. Sometimes I think it's important to
write several ways into a story, so that you have
several semi-finished products rather than facing that FIRST PARAGRAPH. Then you can
steal from yourself and have your own ideas
cross-pollinate each other. You have to discipline
all the parts of your system. It's sort of like
Snoopy talking to various parts of his body that
won't cooperate with him.

Is "Losing It" a tragedy?

It's sad. You don't want to apply the term tragedy
loosely. My editor thought there might be a good
story in aging athletes. The story was interesting
because I thought I would do a great deal of research, and I didn't. I decided that I had been
around baseball for six or seven years, and I was
just going to sit down and think and remember
all the stories just sitting around in my brain.

**"Losing It" comprises a series of terrific an-
ecdotes about aging ballplayers. Where did
you get those?**

The Hank Aaron/Warren Spahn anecdote happened maybe eight months before, out in San
Diego when I was covering something else. I
knew that anecdote fit somewhere but I absolutely did not know where. The Mantle thing
frankly came out of a story that had been done on
Mantle last summer. The DiMaggio story is ancient. The anecdotes about Morgan, Stargell and
Lee are all first hand, gathered during the last
six weeks of the baseball season as I bounced
around covering pennant races. It really irks me
to use dated material. Anything that is not new
to me, I assume is also not new to the reader.
Sports readers are much more omnivorous than

readers of almost anything else. If you've used an anecdote that has been used before, the good reader will pick it up and say, "Oh Gay Talese used that anecdote 10 years ago." I like to think of my pieces as 90 percent fresh to me. Maybe I am rediscovering things. But I want to sit down to write with a sense of near total freshness.

I'm interested in your use of literary allusions in the piece.

Oh, I hate people who use literary allusions. I knew a columnist who just constantly hit people over the head with literary allusions high up in the story, the biggest words he could find in the first six paragraphs, just anything to prove he wasn't a sports writer. Anything to prove that he couldn't tell a simple tale. If Tolstoy can speak simply, then I can try to.

So talk then about your use of literary allusions in "Losing It."

There I thought they were so apt. It's not typical of my work. I had just been reading Keats' letters, and the Keats quote came out of that. It seemed so wonderful to me that I couldn't pass it up. I had also just been reading Dickinson. Those quotes came out of things I was reading that week. I was talking to George Will, the political columnist, and I wondered if he kept a catalogue of quotes or something like that. It was reassuring to find that mostly in his case it's just something that he happens to be reading.

Does it bother you that many people will not understand that your final lines are an allusion to a Dylan Thomas poem?

We vastly underestimate our audience in newspapers. In 11 years I have never had one letter from anybody saying, "What's all this highfalutin' talk?" I get the most touching letters from people who seem semi-literate but who really appreciate what you're doing. I think the fact that people are capable of understanding the Bible, or sensing the emotion in Shakespeare, just proves how far they are above our expectations. If you talk about basic stories, things they can recognize from their own life or comparable experiences, you can reach them. Anybody's critical facilities are a lot greater than their power to create.

What sort of principles and values do you bring to your reporting?

I find that people understand the things they are fascinated with. If you are willing to be technical with athletes, to deal with them at the level at which they do it . . . . If you talk to a golfer about how you extend down the line of a long two-iron shot, you will find that he opens up and goes from the particular to the general in wonderful ways. If you're willing to wade through the particulars of what they do, you'll see the general illuminating principle that's behind it.

Is that how you elicit such provocative quotes?

Right now I'm working on a technical story about club selection at the Masters, a story which seems dull and technical. But it isn't at all. They built the greatest golf course on earth upon an idea of rewards and punishments for the quality of the shot you've hit. The better shot you've hit, the easier the subsequent shot, the more you're rewarded for the previous shot. It will be a nice way of illuminating why the Augusta National is even more special than we think it is.

Yesterday's daily news story was the fact that they changed the grass on all the greens at Augusta. So every reporter is in there saying, "What do you think about the new greens? Did they ruin the course?" Well, they get ordinary quotes because there's resistance when someone comes on in a perfunctory, "You owe me an honest answer" way.

When I talked to Hale Irwin, I talked to him for a long time about the other story I was interested in, the piece on club selection. I'm sure he had spent hours before the tournament thinking about club selection. He could see that I had some concern about golf. And then I said: What do you think of these greens? So he blew the roof off. He said, "They're terrible. What a disappointment. I wouldn't want to be one of the committee members who made this decision." By showing you appreciate the value of what he does, you prove you're not just out to grab a controversial quote. He is going to be more willing to be honest with you about a potentially touchy subject.

Let's move to the Phillies story. Didn't you tell me in a previous conversation that you had to write that story very quickly on a broken machine?

(Laughs.) Well, one that wasn't working any too well. Now that's different. Game story writing is a performance almost like an athletic performance. It's an adrenalin rush. For a game like that I try to arrive early. I don't think about the story at all until I leave the house or the motel for the ballpark. And I start to think about what I'm covering that day. What idea is within the topic? I think in terms of what would the significance of this event be to the people who are in it. What does it mean to Pete Rose to win or lose this game?

What happens when you get to the ballpark?

One thing I like about ballparks is that you can come out two hours before the game and just mill around, sit around, smell the grass, sniff the flavor of the conversation, see how the two teams feel about each other, see what's said around the batting cage when the two teams mingle like zebras around a watering hole. Go to people that you enjoy talking to.

I try never to interview athletes that I don't respect. I've found to my shock that there are probably twice as many people that are worth talking to than I thought there would be on a baseball team. Once you get to know teams better and better, there are probably 10 or 12 people out of 40 or 50. But you can't be everybody's friend. I want to talk to people who want to investigate the experience they're having. I want to talk to people who lead an examined life even if it's only the curve ball they're examining.

What happens when the game starts?

Once the game starts I'm a compulsive note-taker. I keep every pitch, even in a mid-season game. I not only keep a score card, but I also keep every pitch in the game. I have my own system which I wrote about in the September 1980 edition of *Inside Sports*. The story is called "How to Really Watch a Baseball Game." It's a dissertation on how to keep a real scorecard.

Why is it necessary to keep every pitch?

The whole thing is to get your mind to work like the mind of a player on the bench. You're trying to feel the game as they feel it. The only way to do that is to sense as many pitches in the game as possible, so that you know what happened the previous two times Al Bumbry was up. Following the game pitch by pitch, sensing its internal flow has always excited me. That's why baseball is such a good game to cover. There is a visceral dug-out sense of the game. That's why it's so great to talk to players after the game and compare impressions. If athletes believe that you really care about getting the game right, and you aren't merely trying to find an arbitrary hero and goat, but you want the real hero and goat, they'll go along with the program. They're interested in that too. Their criticism as they ride on the bus to the game is much harsher than any criticism you could put on them.

Is it possible to get that kind of contact with the players in a big game like the World Series?

That's one thing that makes the playoffs and World Series so rotten. Because the game starts so late, because there are so many idiots milling around, you can't work the locker rooms right. You want to talk to six players from either team. You've watched the game hard enough to know what to ask so that people who know more can lead you to a sensible position. That sense of ignorance is important, that you can be led to a sensible understanding.

At the Series you can't do that. It's a bullshit performance. It's a tap dance. A lot of rhetoric and fancy writing. That Phillies piece is a perfect example. That's not a good baseball story (laughs) because I didn't talk to anybody. It would have been a much better story if there had been some way to talk to the Phillies.

Did you write that piece in your office?

Are you kidding me? I wrote it in the pressbox. Now, see, during the game I had to write an 1,800 word game story that was finished one minute after the game. I had to write a running story. So for the second story, I took five or ten minutes to clear my mind and started writing. Now while I'm writing they're piping quotes into the pressbox, so I'm listening for the good quotes. Also there are a million people knocking things over, walking behind you, pushing your chair, so it's pretty close to bedlam. That's part of the challenge.